DRAMA

IN

MALTA

(A PERSONAL FLASH-BACK)

by
LT.-COL. H. E. C. WELDON, RA

The Naval & Military Press Ltd

published in association with

FIREPOWER
The Royal Artillery Museum
Woolwich

Published by
The Naval & Military Press Ltd
Unit 10 Ridgewood Industrial Park,
Uckfield, East Sussex,
TN22 5QE England
Tel: +44 (0) 1825 749494
Fax: +44 (0) 1825 765701
www.naval-military-press.com

in association with

FIREPOWER
The Royal Artillery Museum, Woolwich
www.firepower.org.uk

The Naval & Military
Press

MILITARY HISTORY AT YOUR
FINGERTIPS

... a unique and expanding series of reference works

Working in collaboration with the foremost
regiments and institutions, as well as acknowledged
experts in their field, N&MP have assembled a
formidable array of titles including technologically
advanced CD-ROMs and facsimile reprints of
impossible-to-find rarities.

*In reprinting in facsimile from the original, any imperfections are inevitably reproduced
and the quality may fall short of modern type and cartographic standards.*

DRAMA

IN

MALTA

(A PERSONAL FLASH-BACK)

By

Lt-Col H. E. C. WELDON, RA

"For two months during Malta's long air seige, it was anti-
aircraft guns alone which bore the brunt of the attack"

MALTA August 10ᵗ 1942   Lord Gort. V.C.

Presented to Lt. Col. H.E.C. Weldon. R.A who was
the first Brigade Major of 7.L.A.A Brigade—

AUTHOR'S NOTE

A great deal of this personal narrative was originally jotted down in Malta during intervals between the raids. The remainder has been added, and the whole of it revised, while "On Active Service". There lie my excuses for any inconsistencies of style the reader may remark and also for the inclusion of certain episodes to the exclusion of others of at least equal importance. So much happened during the four years I lived out there and now, apart from an invaluable page of dry official statistics, I have only my memory to rely on as a guide. So I deemed it better to make the story a personal one and to tell mainly of those matters, whether military, social or dramatic, of which I had intimate knowledge and which would also serve to give a picture of the background to our lives and battles in that isolated little fortress.

At the same time I have long felt that there should be wider knowledge of the part that was played by the Army in Malta and in particular by the Royal Regiment of Artillery and its brother in arms, the Royal Malta Artillery. It was by these men, without hope or relief or rest, that the constant strain of three years of bombing, isolation and blockade was borne. The epics of naval heroism that ensured the provisioning of Malta and the doughty deeds of the Royal Air Force in its defence are justly renowned through the press and official publications alike. This pen of mine is a very inadequate instrument with which to describe the contribution of the Army as a whole at its true worth. The back-breaking jobs, the constant vigils and spirited defence of those magnificent battalions of Infantry need a scribe of their own. Suffice it for me to say that the names of Hal Far and the Devons, Luqa and the West Kents, Ta Kali and the Manchesters, Safi and the Hampshires, the Dockyard and the Cheshires, to mention only some, will for ever be indissolubly linked in glory and friendship.

But over half of the garrison were "gunners"—English and Maltese—and it is because I am immensely proud of having had the privilege both of serving in Malta during those stirring times and of being a humble member of the Royal Regiment of Artillery that these pages are written in honour of:

The Gunners in Malta, 1940—1943.

ERRATUM

In Index, Chap. VII, for "Crescendo" substitute "Act II".
Chap. VIII, for "Act II" substitute "Crescendo".

In Text, Page 74, Chapter Heading should read "Act II";
Page 83, Chapter Heading should read "Crescendo".

INDEX

Chapter I

Mise-en-Scene

JUDGED in the light of after-events my first view of Malta was symbolic. It came from the deck of His Majesty's Transport Dilwara homeward bound from Hong Kong in February, 1939. The Mediterranean sky was grey and lowering while a sharp icy wind was whipping the waves to angry crests of foam. Rain squalls were frequent and it was as we emerged from one of these that someone cried "Look! There is Malta". We looked and there on our port bow was a small patch of sunlight completely framing a rocky coast line on which appeared to be perched innumerable spires and steeples. Menaced by black clouds all around, Malta stood out bravely in the only shaft of sunlight we were to see that day. That first impression was vivid and ineradicable. It remains still as clear in my memory as my last view of that gallant island some four years later when the aeroplane taking me away from it circled over a little sun-drenched patch of green bravely set in a sea of limitless blue. Into those four eventful years was to be packed all the kaleidoscope of life—happiness and despair, laughter and tears, joy and tribulation, high courage by many and dogged tenacity by all, and last, but by no means least, a sense of inspiration and uplift derived from the knowledge of 'human reactions in the face of gravest peril.

Any community when seen continuously and at close quarters over a space of four years can probably give illustrations of every facet of human existence, but surely those four years from 1939 to 1943 were filled with greater extremes in the human relationships than any other. Malta was a replica of the world at large in the desperate struggle for freedom. She was a replica only in size. The scale of her ordeal and the glory of her eventual emergence from the dark menace that assailed her were unrivalled. From being an easy-living, gay, and some would probably say superficial, Mediterranean station for cheerful naval officers and a sprinkling of the military, Malta became a grim fortress battling for the life-line of the British Empire. Its Service population had previously lived

1

a largely separate existence from its permanent inhabitants, a proud race who had withstood an earlier and vicious siege four hundred years before. But the menace of the common foe united Servicemen and civilians alike in their determination to resist every effort that was made towards their annihilation. For nearly three years the little island, barely eighteen miles by nine in length, was to endure almost continuous attack. The Italian airforce flying high in the azure sky was the first to launch its missiles against the dusty villages and fields below. Ill equipped as it was at the time Malta faced unflinchingly the bombastic threats of Il Duce and the hail of bombs shrieking down from his Italian 'planes. The Italian airforce in itself would have seemed to have been enough for one small island to take on single handed but within six months an even darker threat was to menace its garrison. The Luftwaffe, fresh from its bloody laurels of Guernica, Rotterdam, and the blitz on London, was diverted in great strength to neutralize the so-called "unsinkable aircraft carrier of the Mediterranean". For nearly two years it was to do its worst, but to no avail. Malta stood firm and hit back with all the strength that faith in a cause, trust in God, and eventually a multiplicity of weapons could give.

But death from the air was not the only danger that assailed the island. The sea became perilous for the passage of any ships and hunger began to exert its slow but destroying influence on all. By the heroic measures of our Merchant Seamen and Royal Navy supplies which just sufficed to keep body and soul together were conveyed to the Island. When the stocks had sunk almost to zero the Battle of Egypt was won and Malta, whose presence had so materially contributed to that victory by the diversion of air effort and the sinking of so many Axis ships, was finally relieved. With magnificent resilience the Maltese Islands not only emerged from the very threshold of disaster, but within a few months were to form the stepping-stone to final victory.

It is said that it is the outsider who sees the most of the game, but in the particular instance of this struggle in the Mediterranean that adage did not apply. The strategists and the politicians could regard Malta in its true perspective as a pawn, but a vitally important pawn, in the manoeuvres that were developing before the United Nations were in a position to checkmate the Nazi lust for world domination. Physically cut off from the outside world, with necessarily only very scanty news either being received or despatched, the inside history of all that contributed to Malta's gallant stand was almost a closed book to the world at large. Readers of the newspapers and listeners to the wireless would learn of the thousand and one raids that were launched against the Island; they would listen with bated breath to the accounts of the heroic efforts of the Royal Navy in convoying supplies to its shores, of the Royal Air Force in its long struggle against overwhelming odds, and of the grim resistance with which the gunners and garrison of the Island opposed the might of the Luftwaffe. Hints would be dropped now and then of the desperate straits to which the civilians of that fortress were reduced and the privations that they had to endure. But, though small in size, Malta was a large community and some semblance of a normal background had to be given to these exploits if the sanity of all was to be preserved. The outside world had no knowledge of this normal background, and probably, as it was little different from that of any other community, was not interested at the time when there were so many other more important and more sensational factors to consider. It is, therefore, in an effort to present the day-to-day existence of Malta, in addition to recounting the highlights of its successful defence, that this book is written. It makes no pretence to cover every aspect, for to do that would be to attempt the impossible, but it is hoped that against the thunder of war, destruction and carnage, the reader will be able to descry the efforts of all to adjust themselves to those conditions and, wherever possible, to restore some semblance of normality to their existence.

Owing to the sudden onset of the Albanian crisis the original plans whereby the family would accompany me back to Malta after my leave had to be abandoned, as it was clearly undesirable to risk taking a wife and small child into an area which at any moment might be in the fore-front of a major war. The good ship "Ranpura" in which I travelled, approached Malta in the late afternoon of April 30th. We had seen its rocky coasts and its red topped churches and domes for many hours before we actually turned into the difficult entrance of the Grand Harbour.

As we passed between the famous ramparts of St. Elmo and Fort Ricasoli and approached St. Angelo the whole scene became tinged with an extraordinarily beautiful blue grey light. This light is a characteristic of Malta and occurs almost every evening shortly after sunset. One could never tire of watching it play on the yellow and grey buildings until it fades gradually into the deeper blue of the night. It is like a stage effect, but infinitely more soft and subtle.

Getting off the ship and stepping for the first time into a "dghaisa" in the dark is a nerve racking experience. These little craft, not unlike a cross between a canoe and a gondola, bob about all round the ships and look as if they would capsize at the least opportunity. Surprisingly enough they are very sea-worthy and on many occasions when ferry services cease to run from one side of the harbour to the other on account of rough weather, the "dghaisas" will still be plying. They are rowed across by one or sometimes two men operating paddles and travel at a surprising speed. Having recovered from the bewilderment of this novel form of transport and the shouting and gesticulating crowd that stands on the Customs House steps, the newly arrived visitor to the Island is promptly made to lose all sense of direction by the twists and turns of the roads along which he is conveyed to his hotel or house. This impression is gained because the many creeks and inlets of the two harbours are very similar to each other, and as the roads wind round the narrow promontories of land jutting out like pieces of a jig-saw puzzle, it is impossible for the uninitiated to find his bearings.

There are three main forms of conveyance in Malta, firstly by 'bus, secondly by gharri (which are horse drawn cabs of very ancient vintage and no comfort) and, lastly, one can travel by motor. At first sight Malta would appear to possess no new cars. Every taxi, or even private car, that one sees appears to be in the last stages of dilapidation and repair. In this it follows faithfully the tradition established at almost every large naval station. The British Navy has a flair for getting itself around in cars that seem to be held together solely by string and will-power. This is probably because their stay in such ports is short and intermittent and it would never pay to purchase cars on a long-term policy. My experience on arrival was no different from the above. Having grossly overpaid the "dghaisa" man, as is always the case with a new arrival, I was conveyed in an ancient and rattling taxi around the twisting roads that seemed constantly to return to the same spot.

As everyone knows now Malta and Gozo are the two chief members of the Maltese group of islands—unless by the time this appears in print Pantellaria has been formally added to the list. Lying between Malta and Gozo are the islands of Comino and Cominetto—the latter not much more than a large rock. Comino, however, although sparsely inhabited offers the most wonderful bathing and the water off its coast is world famous for its depth and translucent blue colour. In addition Comino produces the most delicious honey which has a subtle tang all its own. The other satellite is Filfla Island off the south coast of Malta, which is uninhabited and mainly used as a bombing target by the RAF. Gozo, about half the size of Malta and the most northerly of the group, is reached from Malta by steam ferry in a forty-minute crossing which can be very unpleasant. Once safely over, Gozo will be found to be very lovely, being much less built over than Malta and boasting one or two real sandy beaches which are rare elsewhere on those rocky coasts. If ever you should go there make a point of visiting Xlendi (which is breath-taking in its beauty) and see also the new cathedral with its campanili.

Malta itself consists of two distinct portions. The southern half of the Island is rather drab in scenery and, apart from some excellent bathing coves on the south-east coast, has little beauty. This is the industrial half of the Island, and is very largely built over, except in the Delimara peninsula area. It contains all the aerodromes (of which more anon), also Valetta with its twin harbours of Marsa Muscetto and the Grand Harbour with its dockyard, the residential areas of Sliema and St. Julians, and, away to the south-east, the seaplane anchorage of Marsa Scirocco, which the late Lord Strickland tried so hard to persuade the Imperial Government to convert into an empire airways base. Almost all the social and business activity of Malta is centred in or around Valetta and Hamrun.˙ Standing on the high ground near Rabat is Civita Vecchia, or Notabile, or Mdina, the ancient fortress capital of Malta, which boasts all the three names given and marks the beginning of the northern half of the Island. Running right across the Island and dividing it into two are the Victoria Lines, a steep and precipitous escarpment on which were constructed elaborate fortifications during the reign of the great Queen, and which still form a natural defensive line against invasion from the north. Beyond this ridge the country changes, becoming much more broken up and having more vegetation until it peters out past St. Paul's Bay and Mellieha to the rocky and barren Marfa peninsula.

There are very few tarred roads in the Island. Once committed to a side road, the motorist is likely in wet weather to become bogged and in dry weather to be choked by the clouds of dust. Dust is one of the characteristics of Malta. It pervades everywhere and everything and became a serious menace to accurate gunnery during the air-raids. Other characteristics which will probably strike the visitor are firstly the lack of trees or shade except that afforded by buildings and secondly the ubiquitous stone walls in place of our hedges. The stone walls serve more than the normal purpose of marking off one man's field from another. It will soon be noticed how small the area of each field is, many of them not being greater

5

than a large room in an ordinary house. The reason for this is that the soil on the Island is very scarce and shallow and very often there is only four inches of depth before one strikes the hard rock foundations. Legend has it that the soil was brought to the Island in ships and then carried out to the fields. In order to avoid it being blown away into the sea again in the fierce gales that sometimes rage they fenced it in with these stone walls and the smallness of each field is designed also to help prevent its dispersal. In spite of its shallowness the soil is wonderfully productive, several crops a year being culled from it. The methods of farming are primitive in the extreme but there is no doubt that they produce results which would be the envy of farmers in rich agricultural areas in the home country. The glare of the sun in summer is very trying to the eyes and dark glasses are strongly recommended. It is probably this glare beating down on the yellow soil and buildings and being reflected back that is the cause of the exaggerated versions of Malta's hot weather season. In actual fact temperatures are not very high and the heat is often broken by sea breezes, while in winter it can be extremely cold. Taken by and large, however, Malta enjoys a lovely climate and only when the hot damp and depressing "sciroc" is prevalent is there any cause for grumbles.

The Maltese I liked from the very start. They are very proud of their ancestry and origin and woe betide anyone who makes the mistake of thinking they come of Italian stock. Carthage was their place of origin and the Maltese tongue to this day remains a language apart seemingly composed almost entirely of "Xs" and "Zs". Open-handed and generous almost to a fault the Maltese have a highly developed sense of humour which served them well in their times of stress and a cheerfulness of outlook that is infectious. Family life is the mainspring of their existence and the ramifications of all their relationships are not easy to follow in that country of large house-holds.

The Maltese race is somewhat sharply divided between the townsfolk and the country folk. The latter are hard-working, strong and tough individuals, the majority of whom cannot speak any English. The townsfolk on the other hand are highly educated traders and merchants but appear to lack the tough fibre of their country compatriots. The nobility of Malta rests in the hands of a few exclusive families. Elevation to this circle is hard to obtain as marriages generally take place within the charmed circle rather than with individuals outside it. Their houses are a constant source of delight. The normal Maltese house always appears to our standards to be built the wrong way round. Whereas we generally present the best view of our house to the front and the outside world, the facades of Maltese mansions at first sight are generally most unremarkable except for their ordinary and dingy surroundings. But step inside the door which generally leads straight from the dusty street and a vista of loveliness almost always unfurls itself before the eyes. Beautiful gardens, terraces and abundant fruit trees will be seen enclosed by the high walls which form a continuous ring of which the outside wall of the house forms an integral part. The house itself will be found to be spacious, cool and sumptuously fitted and furnished with all the best rooms facing on to the garden or paved courtyard. There is no doubt that this plan does provide a feeling of relaxation and repose in a kingdom of one's own, away from the distractions of the outside world, even in the midst of the crowded and noisy village which forms the surroundings.

There are many reasons suggested as to the origin of the peculiarly ugly head-dress that the Maltese women affect, called "faldettas". They are all made of black material and combine a kind of cloak with a most cumbrous, wide and unwieldy half-moon shaped head-covering. Some authorities say it is a hood of shame worn by all the women after the licentious behaviour of the Turkish soldiery. Others lay the blame on the Knights of Malta themselves and say it was devised to prevent these celibates overlooking the ladies' charms from the ramparts above. However that may be, they are dying out now and few can regret them. Ugly, unmanageable and so uniformly austere of colour and pattern there can have been few thrills in choosing a new one.

Finally a few words on their religion. Malta is a stronghold of Roman Catholicism and has an Archbishop of its own. The power of the clergy is very great and often strongly influences its politics. But it is the simple faith of the people that is so revealing. Churches in almost every town have been built by voluntary labour and voluntary subscriptions. Magnificent edifices they are too, generally dominating their villages so that they are constantly kept in view. Religion and belief in God permeate almost every action and thought of the simple country people. Many will cross themselves and commit themselves to God when they start on a 'bus journey. (I was amazed when I first saw this, but before the journey was far advanced I felt myself in entire agreement with it). But that is only an instance. What is of importance is that their religion is a practical source of help and inspiration to them and

7

was of incalculable value to the whole Island in its hour of trial. One had only to be present in a shelter during a raid and see their little shrines or listen to the masses being said to realise the deep faith that inspired them. Above ground every gun and gun pit manned or occupied by Maltese personnel would have a picture of The Holy Virgin or of Jesus stuck on to it or fixed somewhere where all could see it. Simple and unquestioning was their faith and after bitter trials and tribulations they lived to see it abundantly justified.

*   *   *   *   *   *

My first night in Malta was undoubtedly my most uncomfortable. By some oversight no room had been prepared for me in the Mess so I was taken to a little hotel next door called the Plevna, kept by Peter Tabone and his charming wife. They were full up but eventually I dossed down on a camp bed in a passage where I was eaten by mosquitoes and sandflies all night. I tossed about restlessly as, apart from the physical discomfort, I was slightly apprehensive of meeting the Colonel the next morning for I had never had any experience of Coast Artillery and was supremely ignorant of that highly specialised branch of the Regiment. Sure enough when I met him and tentatively apologised for my lack of knowledge he roared at me

"What? You've never been in Coast Artillery?"

"No Sir," I said, fearing the worst.

"And you don't know anything about it?"

"I'm afraid not, Sir" said I wilting visibly at his stentorian tones.

"Excellent. Neither do I. We'll get on fine", he barked back.

Malta produces many lovely girls but few could combine so much beauty with such spontaneous vivacity in the same degree as Iris Cavanagh-Mainwaring. My wife and I had been great friends with her in Hong Kong where her husband, Ginger, who has performed such prodigies of valour in submarines during this war, was stationed during the time we had been resident there. We had even met in Kobe for a farewell sukyaki party when their homeward bound travel co-incided with our leave in Japan. So I was delighted when I heard her attractive voice (guiltless of any "r"'s) on the telephone inviting me to "a wewy small pahty at my pawents' home". Colonel and Mrs. Denaro had a large house in Valetta overlooking Sliema and Marsamuscetto Harbour and the very small party had, as I suspected would be the case, become a seething mass of sailors, soldiers and civilians crowding out the rooms and overflowing down the stairs. It was a wonderful introduction to Malta and both Iris and her parents made sure I neither lacked company nor drink for a moment. Eventually I staggered away in company with Lt-Commander Bickford, another old Hong Kong acquaintance, to have my first dinner at the Union Club. Bicky was in love— he often was—but this time it was really serious and I'm glad to say that not long after he married the lady of his choice. Alas, their happiness was short-lived as gay courageous Bicky, after exploits with HMS Salmon which made him into almost a national hero, gave his life for his country when he went back to his beloved submarine after gaining accelerated promotion to Commander.

A few nights after the cocktail party I dined with Iris at her own house in company with the Rathbones (he was on the HQ staff) and the Calderons. Commander Philip Calderon and I got on to the topic of acting and from him I learned that the Malta Amateur Dramatic Club was always ready to welcome new enthusiasts. Philip was chairman of the club and Fifi, his wife, although determined not to act, was invaluable as a constructive critic. And so was formed a friendship which lasted right through the siege and through many theatrical productions. The Calderons lived at Attard in the centre of the Island in one of the most charming houses it would be possible to imagine. To knock with those bronze dolphin knockers on the front door of Chez Calderon was the open sesame to a haven of peace and hospitality. The house was all on the first floor overlooking an enclosed courtyard and garden complete with everything down to such minor details as goldfish. During the bombing it had escape after escape from near-misses and blast but survived triumphant to the end.

As the world settled down again to its customary acquiescence in the predatory actions of dictators the Albanian crisis became an accepted fait accompli. Malta breathed again and turned its attention to its own internal politics for shortly the first parliamentary elections since the suspension of the constitution were to take place. Political feeling ran high and was reflected in the local press which certainly fought with the gloves off. The Governor and Commander-in-Chief of Malta was General Sir Charles Bonham-Carter and there was no doubt that he enjoyed the confidence and trust of the people and was largely responsible by his tact and ability for the almost unanimous loyalty with which Malta entered the war. The use of the word "almost" is really unjust as the numbers of those who were actively anti-British were microscopic but, like all minorities, vociferous in their views. They were the followers of Dr. Enrico Mizzi, an ardent pro-Italian. The two main political parties were the Constitutionalist Party led by Lord Strickland and the Nationalist Party with Sir Ugo Mifsud at its head. Sir Ugo was a man of great charm and statesmanship but unfortunately his Party allied itself with the Mizzi adherents. And so in the minds of most the struggle became one between England and Italy and not between two political parties. The results of the election were overwhelmingly in favour of Lord Strickland's Party and Malta's loyalty to England was amply demonstrated. No small part of the credit for this victory is due to the Hon. Mabel Strickland who controlled the party newspaper, the "Times of Malta", and who was later to play such a magnificent role in the victory of Malta over its Axis foes.

All this time I was planning to get Margie and Wendy out to Malta. Everyone else seemed to be doing the same thing and each boat that called in at Malta brought more wives out to be with their husbands for a brief time before the threatened cataclysm broke in the autumn. In July a senior officer returned from London and was quoted as saying on War Office authority that there would be no war because Hitler had accepted the British proposals in toto. This joyful news spread like wildfire and helped to clear any doubts we had so eventually Margie sailed for Malta in the troopship "Somersetshire" leaving Wendy behind in England, as I expected to return home for a course in November in any case. Somehow no one ever thought that there really would be war for how could Hitler risk it against France and the British Navy on one side and Russia on the other? On August 10th Margie arrived looking lovely as ever and we took up residence in a delightful service flat owned by Peter Tabone of the Plevna Hotel which, while not the Ritz, was wonderful value for money. On Tuesday nights there were dances at the Marsa Club—one of the few places which did boast some trees— and it was a fashionable routine to dine first in the open air at the Melita Hotel. We did this, went to dances at the Sliema Club and attended the usual round of bathing and cocktail parties. Thoughts of war receded until like a thunder clap the news of the Russo-German non-aggression pact burst upon the world and altered the whole aspect of the international situation. The prospects of a return home in November became meagre and in all probability Malta would be one of the first places to be attacked. With Wendy in England I felt there was only one course and sadly I returned to our flatlet with a reservation for Margie on a homeward bound ship only eleven days after her arrival. The regiment moved out to War Stations and from the comfort of our flat I was translated to a bare stone room at the top of a steep flight of steps which I immediately christened "Berchtesgaden". And "Berchtesgaden" it remained even when it was converted into the Regimental HQ office.

It was decided that so far as possible normal training would continue so as to disguise our war preparations in some measure. In accordance with this policy we arranged for coast defence practice to take place on August 31st and September 1st. The CRA, Brigadier Paige, attended these and between shoots we were discussing the prospects of war and peace. It was as he was saying that he still thought war would be averted that a soldier came up the steps leading to "Berchtesgaden", saluted and said he had just heard that Germany had invaded Poland. The die was cast and one megalomaniac had plunged the world into years of catastrophe and suffering.

CHAPTER II

Overture

NATURALLY the outbreak of war in England caused an immediate state of emergency to be observed in Malta. All troops were confined to their war stations and every weapon was ready for instant use as no one doubted that Italy would join in and attack the Island without any formal declaration of war. Lookouts scanned the air and sea for the first signs of hostile approach and there was not the slightest question that the garrison—small and inadequate as it was—would hand out a hot reception. Against air attack however, we were woefully weak as there were few AA guns and no fighter aircraft of any description. However, the ranks of the anti-aircraft gunners were swelled in numbers—but not in equipment at first—by the formation of a Dockyard Defence Battery. This battery was composed of volunteers from the employees of the dockyard. The idea was that they would man weapons in the near vicinity of their workshops as part of the general defence of the dockyard which at that time was regarded as the target requiring first priority of defence. Led by Major Bolton they trained enthusiastically and eventually, after Italy's entry into the war, unorthodox in organisation and handling as they were, they manned Bofor guns in the harbour area with great gallantry until finally absorbed two years later in the Maltese 3rd Light AA Regiment, RMA.

The black-out regulations were strictly enforced and the stuffy atmosphere soon engendered in our tiny Mess was not conducive to keeping either alert or good-tempered. However we live and learn and soon managed to let air in without letting light out. In the daytime we were much heartened to see units of the French navy as well as our own as Malta lay on the dividing line of responsibility.

After two or three weeks of this intense inactivity it became apparent that Italy was staying out of the war for the present and a certain amount of leave away from our war stations was allowed, although every dusk and dawn found the defences fully manned and ready for instant action. Training continued all the time and we had constant practice shoots for the coast defences.

Nothing happened however, and one day I wrote a poem of our activities which started off like this—the rest doesn't matter.

Now here is a saga
Of people at Gargur
Defending this island of goats,
Who sit on their bums
And twiddle their thumbs
And shoot at imaginary boats.

It seemed curious to us all that with Malta lying in so isolated a position, and needing shipping to maintain her supplies, no form of rationing of petrol or foodstuffs was then put into force. Outside the actual military posts the outbreak of war had made no difference to the civil population except by enforcing the black-out. The Maltese got over this inconvenience by sitting outside their houses on the pavements and life became very communal. Numerous letters were written to the press complaining of the encouragement to moral laxity that the black-out gave and eventually, whether as a result of these or not, the restrictions were relaxed until midnight. This again seemed a peculiar idea but it was greatly welcomed. Saturday night dances at the Sliema Club and all the usual forms of entertainment soon returned in full force, and the spectre of war receded into the background of life in Malta.

An invitation to me to join the MADC arrived one day signed by Kathleen Warren. I went to Valetta to meet this lady in the Club rooms and so began a friendship that I hope will last for ever. To anyone who knows Malta there is no need to introduce either Kathleen (K) or Ella Warren—her sister. Both are "personalities" and Malta owes much to them both. They are steeped in naval tradition and no Admiral comes ashore there without seeking them out to recall again the days when they were inveigled into MADC productions. Between them they must know more secrets of the Navy than any other pair of sisters, but discretion is their watchword.

The premises of the MADC lie—or rather lay—on the first floor above a particularly smelly wine shop, and I couldn't help contrasting the regal dignity of Miss Warren, as she received me, with the stench of raw wine and the clinking of empty bottles as they were being washed in the courtyard below. K went through all her hoops as acting secretary of the club, in the absence of her sister Ella in England, and as I watched and listened visions of Ruth Draper opening the bazaar and conducting the tourists leapt to my mind. Eventually I risked it and told K that I thought she was giving a very good performance whereupon we both laughed and went out for a drink and any officialdom in our relations was banished for ever.

The first and most pressing need in the way of entertainment was for concert parties to tour the isolated forts and gun-positions and I promised to do all I could and also to try and write a scene or two. Only a few days later while crossing the Sliema harbour by ferry I ran into Susan Ennion whom I had met first a few days earlier at a dinner party. She was just off to a committee meeting to decide what play they were going to do round about Christmas time. It would probably be "French Without Tears". This news thrilled me, as ever since I'd seen an amateur production of that play in Hong Kong I had hankered after playing the part of Commander Rogers—that seemingly so obtuse and cantankerous sailor of Terence Rattigan's creation. It never occurred to me for one moment that I would ever play it but I made up my mind to attend the audition and have a shot at it. Never have I been so nervous as on the day of that audition. K and Susan were among those sitting in judgement but someone introduced me to Jean Martyn who had been a leading light in repertory in England. We both nervously made small talk of the most stilted type and agreed that auditions in cold blood were ghastly ordeals. Jean is one of the most attractive and gayest people it is possible to meet and she combines those attributes with a superfluity of modesty that hides an actress of outstanding talent and an artist to her finger-tips. But on this first meeting between us neither of us shone to great advantage.

The audition dragged on and, feeling that I had boobed my bits, I left somewhat despondent of my chances against the efforts of several naval officers who were also vie-ing for the part. In the middle of dinner that night K told me that only two definite allocations of roles had been decided upon—Jean Martyn as Jacqueline and myself as the Commander. We must have been sitting in the lucky corner. Later Susan—who had been well known on the London stage before her marriage—was chosen for Diana, and K was elected the producer.

Meanwhile, although the war had not yet touched Malta its ravages had spread over Poland and the world was being shocked by the inhuman treatment meted out to that gallant people. History can have no finer page in its book than the maintenance of the national spirit of Poland and the steadfast determination on the part of everyone in that country never even to temporise with their oppressors. Spontaneous tributes were paid by peoples all over the world and money was freely given to charities and organisations formed to alleviate the distress of the afflicted refugees. Malta proved no exception to that rule and it was arranged that a gala charity concert should be given in the Royal Opera House Valetta under the patronage of His Excellency the Governor and that the proceeds should be donated to the Polish Refugee Fund. The concert was to have both English and Maltese artistes performing and K was asked to provide the English numbers. She asked me to help by providing a musical scene. I had been doing a "turn" of that sort in the concert parties but for this I devised a new scene, based on the most famous songs of Noel Coward, and persuaded Dorothy Freemantle to appear in it with me. She had a highly trained operatic voice and was an excellent actress also, as was shown by the fact that she had played Polly during part of the run of the Beggars Opera in London. Unfortunately she was not very good at remembering the exact times of rehearsals which had to be strictly adhered to if Maestro Bellizzi, the musical director, was to get through his day. Before the dress rehearsal I felt we were under-rehearsed but worse was to come as on the day of the dress rehearsal I caught a "stumer" of a cold and lost my voice. I was anxious to cancel our scene if possible but alas, the running order of the revue precluded any chance of that merciful release. However, Dorothy Freemantle was in superb voice and the rehearsal passed off moderately satisfactorily. However, I still longed for one more rehearsal with the orchestra but we could not fit it in anywhere so I looked forward to the morrow with gloomy foreboding. That night there were military manoeuvres and the CO did one of those things that one remembers with gratitude for ever. He ordered me to bed and sat up all night doing my work as adjutant so that I might have some chance of singing the next night at the opening performance. Alas, my voice disappeared completely and I could only croak miserably at the opening although a last-minute strong black coffee and brandy kindly handed to me by Harry Cachia, the Maltese baritone, did help to a considerable extent. The next day Dorothy sang and acted beautifully and my voice was coming back so the scene went quite well but I shall always look back on that first gala performance with feelings akin to nightmare.

It was an inauspicious start but it's an ill wind and that concert introduced me to a Maltese lady of infinite charm, looks and talent with a voice like an angel. Ada Bonello was famous in Malta for she had sung the leading parts in many light operatic and operatic productions and had reached a zenith when she was chosen to play the title role of "The Belle of New York", before their present Majesties. She has a voice which can range from the merest whisper to full volume and never once does it lose its sympathetic quality. With her looks and infectious charm allied to those golden notes she quickly captures any audience and I am convinced she would have created a sensation on the London stage. Unfortunately she is a devoted mother and wife and would never think of sacrificing her family ties for the rewards of fame. In this concert she was singing a song from "The Dancing Years" as one number. It transpired that for both of us it had been the last show we had seen in London and incidentally I was to see it again still running in London nearly five years later. We discussed music and the stage in all its forms as we waited in the wings. Some weeks later Ada and her husband, Walter Bonello, who also had a pleasant voice and had played opposite her on many occasions, came with our concert party to the gun positions on several occasions. Ada could sing anything to the soldiers and she never played down to them in her selection of songs. The result was that they clamoured for more and more. Arias from "Tosca" and "Madame Butterfly", lilting songs by Lehar and Strauss, melodies by Novello and Hermann Lohr all were vociferously received in turn and she even brought new meaning to the hackneyed "Roses in Picardy". Two and a half years later it was my proud privilege to persuade Ada to come and sing to Malta in a series of broadcasts when the Island was at the height of its peril, and any form of entertainment or relaxation was hard to devise and therefore sorely needed.

Just a word now on our concert parties. Twice weekly the small band of enthusiasts bundled into cars of all shapes and sizes, stuffed costumes, scenery and make-up into dicky seats and along running boards and trundled off to some lonely military post. We played in regular theatres, in huts, in tents, on bare boards and sometimes on mud. Sometimes we changed in lorries or in tents and sometimes there wasn't so much as a screen to separate the ladies from the gentlemen. Inspired by the enthusiasm of K Warren we all gladly gave up a great deal of our free time, re-arranged watches and duty days in order to try and bring entertainment to the troops. It was well worth the effort too, as our shows did seem to be appreciated by them. Changes of cast were of course constant and one never knew what sketches one might have to play in without warning. It certainly made for alertness of mind and body as we all had to do our own scene-shifting too. From the moment of arrival to that blessed instant in the Mess when one sank into a chair or onto a bench with a glass in one's hand there was no rest for the workers and certainly no peace for the wicked. All my spare time away from the headquarters was given up to these concert parties and to the rehearsals for "French Without Tears" which had now been fully cast. The play was beginning to take shape when the CO decided to move the regimental office back to Tigne as the state of vigilance had been further relaxed owing to Italy's inactivity. The Mess at Tigne was full up mith many Maltese officers being taught the mysteries of anti-aircraft artillery and so I had to billet myself out. Luckily at this very moment Marjorie Bryant, wife of the ace submarine commander Ben Bryant, vacated her bedroom in the Ennion household and left for England with her baby. So I moved in just before Christmas and still feel a sense of proprietary pride from this close association whenever I read of Ben's gallant feats.

CHAPTER III

Prologue

STAYING near Valetta with the Ennions was very convenient, as just at this time rehearsals for "French Without Tears" were becoming more and more hectic. In addition to her duties as housewife, mother of two children, Secretary of the Naval Wives Association, and rehearsing for the leading part in "French Without Tears", Susan was also doing long hours of ciphering work for the Navy, necessitating her losing a nights sleep twice a week. In any spare hour that she had, she was still taking part in our concert parties. Nobody can stand such pressure of work for long and, sure enough, ten days before Christmas and a week before the production was due, she caught a chill. Within twenty-four hours this had turned into jaundice and our leading lady was obviously unfit to play on the opening night. After every possibility of obtaining a substitute had been explored in vain, the production had to be postponed until January 11th.

Christmas passed off uneventfully and very quietly, with the exception that I received the glad news that Margie and Wendy would be coming out early in the New Year. Susan rapidly threw off her attack of jaundice and strictly against doctor's orders agreed to play on January 11th. In the meantime I was much occupied in house-hunting and was eventually lucky enough to find a beautifully furnished flat overlooking the sea at Tigne and even a maid to run it. With the advice of Susan from her sickbed and the active help of the maid, I managed to get the entire flat completely furnished and victualled before the arrival of the family. In a last moment's brilliant inspiration, I even remembered an ironing board. The imminent arrival of a small child who had been used to nothing but the best Devonshire cream and fresh milk at the glorious home of her devoted grandparents, provided a problem in this land of Malta where condensed and goats' milk were the orders of the day. I laid in an immense stock of the most expensive type of tinned milk which was guaranteed to be lapped up by any child. At the first taste I was firmly informed that she didn't like it.   We tried every expedient but quite obviously Maltese milk supplies were not up to the standard she had been used to, until, finally, in desperation, I bought a carton of pasteurised goats' milk and thrust that at her.   To my vast relief she lapped it up and from that moment there was no trouble.

Of course, the Egyptian Mail line by which they were travelling would choose January 11th of all days for their arrival.   This meant a frantic rush to collect them and their luggage from off the ship, put them in the flat and organise myself, my costumes and my make-up in time for the opening curtain.   John Ennion stepped nobly into the breach and escorted my wife to dinner and the theatre while his wife and I had a hurried sandwich meal while making up.

Of all the places in which "French Without Tears" has been a success, I am sure none has rivalled Malta.   Our press notices were "raves".   The predominantly Naval audience there enjoyed every jest at their expense to the full.   Susan not only looked a picture but fully justified the committee's decision to postpone the play until she could play, while Jean Martyn, who from the first rehearsal never put a foot or gesture wrong, gave a most beautiful and tender performance as Jacqueline. We played for three nights and the vast Opera House was packed on each occasion, the Club clearing a record profit.   On the first night Robert Flemyng, who had played the part of Kit Neilan over a thousand times in the London production, passed through on war service, came backstage to see us all and we imbibed sherry in my dressing-room.

Brigadier Paige—the · C.R.A.—having seen the London production had told me he would not attend any amateur performance.   However, he found himself in a dinner party, given for it on the opening night and so willy nilly he had to go on to the show.   The next night he took a box and said later that he had enjoyed the performance even more than in London.   This was music in our ears as he was a critical authority on matters appertaining to the stage.   My own personal cup of happiness was filled to the brim when the Governor sent round a special message saying that he hoped that every Naval Officer would come and see themselves on the Opera House stage.   But the major share of all the credit was due to K. Warren who had been so indefatigable in conducting and arranging rehearsals to· fit in with our various hours of freedom and whose methods of production had kept the whole cast a happy team throughout.

Life in Malta was still unruffled on the surface, but HM submarines were constantly active under it.   We made great friends with a certain Submarine Officer of large girth and proportions and had many a good evening with him. One day while showing us over his command he proceeded to state that he could get through the conning tower and crash dive within one minute. Looking at him we doubted it and much point was given to our doubts some months later when his submarine was rammed and all aboard her were taken prisoner.

In the intervals of work and playing golf and tennis and attending the constant round of cocktail parties, we produced a revue which earned more money for Naval charities. In this review ocurred the then inevitable scene of Lord Haw-Haw broadcasting. We had great good luck, as on the opening night HMS Ark Royal slipped into Malta, and we were able to have a curtain line of Lord Haw-Haw asking his usual question, "Where is the 'Ark Royal'?". Richard Bright, who had often performed with the BBC, was one of the leading characters in this revue. I think I have never played with anyone who was so thoughtful for his fellow actors and yet so clever an artist in himself. He was of tireless strength, both before and behind the curtain. Another member of the cast was Ann Heffernan, whom I last saw in London playing the part of a nun in John Gielgud's production of "Cradle Song". I couldn't help contrasting her saintly demeanour then with the daring dress and abandon with which she put over "My Heart Belongs to Daddy" in our revue.

It wasn't long after that revue was finished that the monitor HMS Terror tied up at some moorings in Marsamuscetto Harbour. She obviously wasn't there for fun and her anti-aircraft armament was perpetually trained upwards. Practices took place with her big guns in co-operation with the coastal defences and very soon it was realised that the wings of war were brushing close to Malta, and Italy was mobilising to take her stand by the side of her Axis partner. Rumour succeeded rumour—such of HM ships as still were based on Malta left for Alexandria — the naval staff vacated the Castille and Head-quarters Malta Command prepared to move to their War Headquarters.

At this juncture, the Governor and Commander-in-Chief, General Sir Charles Bonham-Carter, fell ill with pneumonia and for a time his life was despaired of. In fact it was only saved by the rushed arrival by air of medical supplies and equipment from England. It was obvious after so serious an illness that for a long time he would be unfit to take over the arduous duties of Governor in an area that was likely so soon to be subject to annihilating attack by the Axis. But a substitute was sent out whose name will be associated forever with the heroic defence of that Island. General Dobbie, who had earlier been GOC at Singapore, arrived to take over the duties of Acting Governor. Fearless and full of righteous conviction in the justice of the Allied cause, General Dobbie immediately took a firm stand and became almost over-night a figurehead to whom Malta looked for salvation. His stirring broadcast that "Malta could and would be defended" was the first really positive indication of a determination to hold the Island at all costs and gave much cheer to garrison and people alike. But words were not sufficient for him. Deeds had to come too, and he immediately set about obtaining anti-aircraft defences and an increased garrison for that outpost of Empire. The time before him was short, but his energetic representation ensured that plans were made for Malta's reinforcement and adequate defence, and these seeds were to yield their full harvest before the sternest part of the test assailed the defenders.

Shortly after this broadcast, the Government warned us to send our families home while it was yet possible. So many false alarms had occurred in the past that even at this late hour there were many who doubted the necessity for this step. There were the very real hazards of the sea to be faced if we sent our families away whereas as yet the Italian menace was only a threat. But the threat grew more and more bombastic and the strength of Malta was woefully weak to pit against the vaunted Fascist might. After much searching of heart practically everyone took the sad decision to evacuate their families and finally on the night of May 20th, 1940, I stood watching the dim outline of S.S. Oronsay merge into the blackness of the night— taking two thousand of Malta's defenders' loved ones back to England—while the chariots of War rumbled nearer with the dawn.

Packing off the family by the good ship "Oronsay" was not the end of my troubles. There still remained all the contents of the flat to be sorted out and packed and a Maltese maid had to be left in charge of this somewhat important work while I, in company with the rest of the Regiment, dashed off to war stations once more. In any odd moments that were free to me I settled up the household debts and tried to supervise the final packing of the furniture and all the clothes that had been left behind. I thought I had sorted everything out correctly, but our Maltese maid felt that she knew better and that the china was of more value than the clothing. The result was that when the majority of the boxes arrived safely in England, all the china was intact in the steel lined chests and what clothing had not been eaten by rats had been devoured by moths.

We tried, in spite of dwindling transport and dwindling numbers, to keep the concert parties going. I think the last few of these must have been rather sorry spectacles, as everybody was doubling for everybody else and members of the cast were sometimes recalled in the middle of the performances. We travelled round in a Scammel diesel lorry in order to save petrol and altogether it was no picnic. However, enjoyment of anything always depends on its availability and as no other form of entertainment was provided for the troops even our somewhat pitiful efforts seemed to be appreciated.

Still there was no definite sign that Italy had decided to throw in her hand with the Axis. However, all leave was stopped, men were only allowed away from their war stations for a maximum of four hours at a time and everyone had to be present and on the quivive by dusk.

The CO left to go to a staff appointment at home and was succeeded by Lt-Col C. J. White, MC, with whom I was to serve in varying ratios of rank for the next three years. Most of the time I said "Sir" to him, for a short time we were level and once for a short fortnight he said "Sir" to me, out of which we both got considerable amusement and we hope the Treasury derived some profit.

Meanwhile things were happening with devasting swiftness in Europe. The Maginot Line had proved the white elephant that nobody had suspected it to be and the German Blitzkrieg was in full force.

To us in the isolated little Island, secure in the knowledge that even if Italy did come in, Algeria and Tunisia were French and would be used to base fighters for our defence, the prospect of a tottering France merely seemed one of academic interest and pity. Some people had questioned whether the French would survive this concentrated attack, but to us ignorami the recall of Marshal Petain with his famous watchword of "they shall not pass" was a sure sign that the French meant to fight on, and we all too easily forgot his Fascist connections in Madrid. Thus it was a considerable shock to learn that France was sueing for a separate armistice. But even so, the blind stupidity of the English in their constant refusal to know when they are beaten asserted itself and most of us said, "Well, that's that. Now we can get on with the job".

On a very hot day we were all strolling about inside the fort which was the Headquarters of the Regiment, when a signaller burst out from the exchange and announced that

Mussolini had declared his intention of joining next day with Germany in the coup de grace on France and Great Britain. This meant us, and it gave us a thrill to hear the instantaneous cheers that went up from all the troops when they heard the news. Since 1935 there had been false alarm after false alarm; the troops had stood to their guns, beach posts had been manned and long hours spent on watch at frequent intervals only for the scare to die down and relapse into the limbo of the forgotten past. No sooner had everyone taken up the old routine of life than yet another bombastic utterance from Il Duce sent everyone scuttling back to their war stations. Latterly, of course, these scares had been frequent and everyone was fed up with them. Therefore, it was with a feeling of real relief that the pitifully inadequate garrison of Malta received the news that at last the fight was on.

We "stood to" that evening and I remember how clearly in the evening sunset the coast of Sicily and the snow-capped top of Mount Etna stood out. However, that was all that could be seen apart from HMS Diamond patrolling round the Island in search of submarine contacts. For lack of anything better to do we decided to report the presence of Mount Etna up to the Harbour Fire Commander and sent a message "Hostile Volcano in sight". This unfortunately caused an immediate flutter as it was mistaken for the Italian cruiser "Vulcano" and everybody there "stood to" with even extra purpose. However, the twilight deepened into that familiar blue light which always envelopes Malta just before nightfall and excitedly we went back to the Mess to have a cup of cocoa—or perhaps something stronger—and wait to see what the morrow would bring.

Chapter IV

Act One

I am not sure that many of us slept very well that night. We had been filled up with all sorts of stories of what bombing could do to us and we also knew how very thin we were on the ground should the Wops attempt an invasion. The power of Fascism looked formidable and we were not to know then that it was only a bubble that could be broken with the greatest of ease. As a result most of us were awake even before the dawn "stand to" which passed off without incident.

So far war seemed very peaceful and we returned to our rooms for our morning shave and breakfast. The power for the working of the guns was provided by an engine within the fort which also provided current for lighting the rooms. Some of us were proud possessors of electric razors and we had to perform the shaving rite during the time that the engine was kept running in order that the guns could be instantly serviced as the CO objected to turning on a 40 horse-power engine to allow his officers to shave.

At about a quarter to seven on June 11th, the siren began wailing. It is hard to remember now amongst all the excitement of that first day, but I am almost certain that the first raid on Malta began with the prolonged sounding of the "All Clear". Everybody realised what it meant, however, and I came out of the wash place to find three Maltese workmen trying to crowd into the lavatory to get some shelter. I told them not to be stupid and that we should be perfectly all right, although I must say that I didn't feel at all convinced of it. I then walked through the ante-room to see if I could get a view of the 'planes coming in and found one of our Majors complete with tin hat and a stick in his mouth, sitting under the dining room table; a position which looked so undignified that I just roared with laughter and after that one experience he never adopted it again.

Very soon the hum of the aeroplanes was heard and high up in the sky like little silver fish came the first bombers on

Malta. They seemed to be a little bit away from us although we, as the hub of the coast defence, fully expected to be the first target in preparation for the anticipated invasion. Only a few days before a lone Alalittoria 'plane had suddenly altered its course on its regular journey from Malta to Naples and had swept low over Gargur. That had seemed to us highly significant. In addition to that, the entrance to the fort had a permanent arch, the only one of its kind in Malta. We beseeched the CO to have this removed at once, but he refused, curtly saying he had designed it himself. However, it was not our turn this time and soon we heard the shriek of falling bombs and saw the pulverised limestone of the buildings in the dockyard area thrown into the sky in that thick dust cloud that we were to view all too often during the years to come.

Meanwhile an excited telephone call came from Fort Binjemma, which lay on the far side of the Island and was screened from Valetta by hills.

"Has there been a coast defence action?" telephoned the Fort Commander.

"No", said I, who was on the telephone at the other end.

"Oh, I thought I heard a noise like gunfire", came the reply.

"Well Valetta has been bombed".

"This is no time for unseemly levity", was the Fort Commander's irate reply, for which he had to apologise some short time later.

Many stories have been written of the first day of raiding on Malta. In all we had eight attacks practically all of them being concentrated on the area between the dockyard and Luqa aerodrome. Civilian casualties were fairly heavy, but the raids in themselves were a typical augury of the Italian war effort. They were half-hearted, and were never pressed home in any strength. In fact they were really just what was needed at the smallest cost possible to stir up the animosity of the people of Malta against the Italians. The story might possibly have been different if in that first day, or even the night before, they had raided the Island with the full strength of the Regia Aeronautica.

For months now the anti-aircraft gunners had been sitting at their guns, constantly on the alert for a surprise assault before a declaration of war, as was the fashion in those days. But now they had had warning and they seized their chance with both hands. In fact one could safely say that never in the field of human conflict had so many shells been shot up in so short a time by so few. Fortunately some of the 'planes flew into them which must have caused the Italians some losses as nothing but a reconnaissance 'plane came over the Island for the next twenty-four hours. That 'plane was promptly shot down by the gunners so it was unlikely that the Italians learnt much of what they had achieved which, in so far as damage to the military effort was concerned, was nil.

I travelled down with the Colonel to the other end of the Island near Hal Far that day and we stopped at a house which had been hit by a bomb. We enquired of the proprietor whether he had suffered much damage.

"Oh no", he said cheerily, "It killed one of my children and spoilt a lot of furniture, but we are quite all right". In those days both were easily replaced. Furniture got very scarce later on.

The whole tone of the population was very cheerful. The Governor's prompt action in locking up the Lord Chief Justice, who was a noted pro-Italian, and his stirring broadcast on the night before war began had given great confidence to the defenders and inhabitants alike.

And now let me digress for a few minutes to tell of undoubtedly the three heroes of the first day, who captured the admiration of all and whose story will always resound when tales of gallant deeds are told. They are "Faith", "Hope" and "Charity", three Gladiator aeroplanes left behind in boxes in the dockyard by H.M.S. Glorious when she sailed away to northern waters on that journey which was to end so tragically. Stationed in Malta were pilots who had flown London flying boats, Seal aircraft and such like crates that at best could seldom exceed a hundred miles an hour even if they flapped their wings their hardest. Malta had no fighters but these boxes had been discovered in the dockyard and so these lads turned themselves into fighter pilots. Fully to appreciate the extent of their endeavours you must realise that the Gladiator was not as fast on the level as the Italian bomber and that he could only just climb to the height from which the Italians bombed if he left the ground immediately the attack was suspected and caned his engine all out during the approach of the bombers. If he could get above them he had a faint chance of catching them in his downward dive. All this needed immense guts and great judgement and it was fortunate that the Island was well equipped with radio location which enabled it to get early information of aerial activity.

That particular day as the CO and I were proceeding to Hal Far we saw them taking off for the fifth time that morning against a raid that was estimated at over forty 'planes. The raid turned out to be smaller than that but even so those pilots did not hesitate to take the air against such insuperable odds. Eighteen months later I was to see two Spitfires take off and battle in the air against an approaching German raid of one hundred and forty. Admittedly the numerical odds against these two were even greater, but they did at least have armament which their opponents respected and I class those two examples of courage as equal and in the highest category it is possible to imagine. Day after day with our hearts in our mouths we used to follow those three little 'planes as they spiralled up into the clear blue sky high above us. Everyone of the pilots was known to us and we used to follow their manoeuvres with breathless interest. When they disappeared out of view in pursuit of some of the retreating bombers— remember, as I have explained, they did not have time to get them coming in—the whole Island used to stand and wait for their return, counting them in until all three had safely landed. For many weeks these three Musketeers formed the sole aerial defence of Malta and it seemed that they bore a charmed life. Early on in the attacks the Italians did not bother to escort their bombers, but so well did these three Gladiators perform that after a bit the usual spearhead of five Savoya 79s began coming over heavily escorted by midget-like CR 42s and Macchis.

There is bound to be an end to this life of adventuring against hopeless odds and in due course Ronny Keeble paid forfeit for his daring in a terrific dog fight with an Italian fighter. The two of them came crashing to earth and one of Malta's gallant three was lost. The other two survived to the end. One of the 'planes was eventually put to experimental use and had its engine power boosted up to a speed that had never before been attempted by a Gladiator, but by then the Hurricanes had arrived and the day of these lightly armed Knights of the air had passed. They had done their work all too well as they had forced the Italians to escort their bombers before the first flight of twelve Hurricanes landed in Malta. What carnage would have been wrought had those fat silvery Savoyas suddenly been faced with twelve eight-gun Hurricanes.

However, now to return to earth. Invasion scares were frequent and all the defenders were constantly on the alert for the least sign of in-shore reconnaissance or the landing of Fascist agents on Malta. To such an extent was this pursued that Fort Bingemma greeted their beer lorry which arrived rather late one evening with a fusillade or rifle fire and their supplies of beer were threatened with being cut off in consequence.

Months of constant vigil do undoubtedly produce a state of tension in the mind in which the most ordinary things of every day life assume hitherto unknown proportions. Let me tell you of one incident which actually occurred in our own fort. It was the night that the Italians first took to night raiding and for some reason confusion again reigned in the alarm system of the Island. Every time the "All Clear" sounded a bomb dropped and every time the alarm went, the air above seemed to be completely free of all hostile noises. To such an extent was this carried on that eventually Headquarters became confident that there was an enemy agent signalling to the bombers when the alertness of the anti-aircraft defenders was at all relaxed. An urgent telephone message was broadcast to all posts warning them to keep a look-out for any suspected signalling. The look-outs at Fort Gargur strained their eyes and there, sure enough, not far from the fort was a light signalling. Some even said that they could read some of the letters that he was sending out, but as it was apparently in Italian code this could not be checked. The light was greeted with a fusillade of rifle and machine gun fire, but continued to signal undisturbed. It was then decided that a patrol should be sent out to capture this signaller and it was agreed that the man who could best be spared and who was the most suited to lead the patrol was the Regimental Sergeant Major. He led his party through a gap in the barbed wire defences, which we had hitherto considered impenetrable, and proceeded to worm his way on his stomach towards the source of the signalling. Meanwhile, two gunners, on their own initiative, had found another way through the barbed wire and these two parties met quite close to the place where the signals were coming from and each mistook the other for the enemy. Finally a hoarse command from the watch tower in the fort persuaded them to cease attacking each other and to capture the enemy agent who must be within five yards of both parties. At last the lights went out and the patrols returned in triumph bearing with them a glow worm which continued to wink happily within the precincts of the fort.

The outbreak of war had prevented me from going to the Staff College at Haifa for which I had been selected as it was obvious (a) that nobody could get there except by air, and we did not possess the aeroplanes and (b) that officers could ill be spared from the meagre garrison that was present. So I stayed on as Adjutant and learned how much can be done to keep up the morale in the face of inactivity by enthusiasm on the part of the CO. One of the complaints of the troops was lack of mail from home. It wasn't fully appreciated by us how desperately short England was of aeroplanes of all kinds and it was universally considered that at least one 'plane might be spared to visit Malta, if only once a week, with news of their families who were then beginning to face the ordeal of the Battle of Britain. No newspapers ever arrived in the Island and the only sources of information were the BBC broadcasts (which proceeded to assure them every day that four hundred German bombers had caused no damage whatever in England), and the "Times of Malta" which would only print the official news releases which were hardly less misleading. The difficulties of instituting a regular mail service were undoubtedly great but it is doubtful whether they were so insuperable as appeared.

The question of mail cropped up again and again during this siege and one realised the vital importance to the morale and well-being of any troops, and particularly those of isolated garrisons, that the regular arrival of mail implies.

Early in August the CO handed me a letter which had come in from Headquarters Malta Command saying that I was to be posted there as GSo3 (Operations), and would, therefore, have to leave the Regiment. I was sincerely sorry to do so, but it would provide an opportunity for becoming acquainted with staff work and possibly later on getting to the Staff College which had been denied me as a result of Mussolini's "mare nostrum" policy.

Compared with the extremely comfortable little room in the new Mess at Gargur which had just been built for us, the first quarter that I occupied at Headquarters Malta Command was a considerable comedown. It consisted of a flimsy little hut once used as a medical inspection room perched on the top of the ramparts and gave one the impression that it was the centre of the bullseye for any night bombing attack. However, the Headquarters was rapidly expanding and soon even that small place was used for other purposes and I managed to rent a small flat on the eighth floor of a building in Valetta. This gave one a wonderful view of all air raids if one did not look down or allow one's imagination any play.

My first experience of staff work in a large Headquarters was of bewilderment at all the various channels that one had to explore in order to produce the answer to any problem. The regimental soldier when he condemns the workings of the staff forgets that the problem that he puts up is his own particular problem that affects him from one particular aspect. The solution to that problem may well embroil half a dozen various branches of a large staff and it is not always that the question he has forwarded up for decision is the only one which is occupying their attention at the time. It was as a result of a poem I wrote on the intricacies and delays of staff work which is too technical for reproduction here, that a vogue was created in the composition of poetry which even extended to some official replies. On one occasion one of our clerks who had been requested to stay in on his off day as there was extra work to do, complained that if this was often to be the case he would be unable to fulfil his social obligations. The GSO2 referred this to me for my report, suggesting that it might be done in rhyme and this was the result, which I believe is still in the official files:—

A SOCIAL OBLIGATION

When he signed his attestation
    And he vowed he'd dedicate
His whole life to the nation
    And the service of the State,
By some mental aberration
    He forgot he had a date
A most important assignation
    That really couldn't wait.

Without a moment's hesitation,
    For he feared he might be late
For his social obligation
    (And he never tempted Fate),
He typed a passionate oration
    To the Secretary of State
Asking for a dispensation
    To meet his chosen mate.

The utter consternation
    That thence did emanate
Was mixed with admiration
    That nothing could abate.
For his social obligation
    Was an urge to procreate
And in that consummation
    Do his duty to the State.

It was down at Command Headquarters that I first came into contact with senior officers of the Royal Navy and the Royal Air Force. I was very lucky in these first contacts as the Vice Admiral Malta was Admiral Sir Wilbraham Ford who was a bluff sailor of the type of which England's Navy has been made for years. He never minced words and his staff considered him hopelessly indiscreet, but when you came to analyse what he told you, you never found that he had given anything away that you would not have known from the ordinary public channels within a very few hours. His cheeriness and constant good humour were largely responsible for preserving the good atmosphere that existed in spite of hot weather, sciroc, grim quarters and bombing. Particular butts of his humour were the then CRA and the GSO2, the latter an officer of very upright ideals and religious convictions. Nothing delighted Admiral Ford more than to pull his leg and try to shock him. One day a postcard of a beautiful Hollywood film star was discovered under the pillow of the GSO2 and on opening the drawer of his desk he found yet another one with a loving message inscribed on it. He tried to hush this up but too many people were in the know and eventually he came into our office and accused us of planting them on him. Discreet investigation disclosed, however, that the Admiral had been seen coming away from the GSO2's office shortly before the discovery of the lovelies and this report in rhyme was enabled to see the light of day.

Headquarters is shaken and shocked to the core,
    Its bachelor status degraded
By film-stars and lovelies that never before
    Its virginal pillows invaded.
Propaganda and leaflets have dropped from the skies
    And maybe some other things too,
But now all the Staff are expressing surprise
    Amazed at the GSO2.
As they watched him quite placidly eating his lunch
    None could have possibly said
That up in his room in a nice little bunch,
    Were photos of film-stars, in bed.
He denied that he knew them and said: "It is clear
    This is one of the Admiral's tricks,
I've been faithfully married for many a year
    And don't really care for the flicks.
I'm indifferent to Garbo or any film-star
    Whose pictures incline to be rude,
I'm not even keen on that Hedy Lamarr
    Who dashes about in the nude. ·
From this grave moral stigma I wish to be freed
    And be able to lift up my head
And the problem I wish to be solved with all speed
    Is, "Who put the girls in my bed?"
The D.S.O. put on his scarlet lined cloak
    And stuck on his favourite beard,
Then cleverly thought "Where there's fire there is smoke"
    And off to the Admiral he steered.

Explaining his mission, he said: "You will see
   The G.2's poor wife is at home
And in spite of their leaflets THESE beauties won't be
   Distributed gratis by Rome.
And so I've been ordered to make a good search
   And seek out the cunning man who
Has most reprehensively tried to besmirch
   The morale of the G.S.O.2".
The Admiral said: "Ah! I think you will find
   That some of 'G' Staff are in league"
But after that statement he flatly declined
   To unravel the dreadful intrigue.
The D.S.O. questioned each G.S.O.3
   But they'd learned all their answers off pat,
He even suspected his own G.O.C.
   (But he kept very quiet about that).
But no one was found who could justly be blamed
   (Some thought it was H.Q., R.A.),
But now the G.2's universally famed
   For his photo of sweet Alice Faye.

Admiral Ford had it copied and distributed to many units of the Fleet which must have mystified them considerably. One word of explanation is necessary: DSO was the Defence Security Officer, Colonel Bertram Ede, and we always referred to him and his officers as the "cloak and dagger boys".

Part of my duties as GSO3 (Operations) lay in ensuring that the Island was in a fit state of preparedness against gas attack. All sorts of horrible stories were going around of what the Axis gas bombs and spray could do to us and the Island became very gas-minded. The General instructed me to run a series of surprise exercises in an endeavour to gauge the instinctive reactions of everyone to an onslaught by gas. One of the buildings scheduled for these visitations was Malta Command Headquarters. Within this Headquarters there were two alarms, one the gas alarm and the other the anti-parachutist alarm. On the day of the exercise sure enough some private in the Royal Corps of Signals discovered red spots upon the green indicator denoting the presence of gas. With admirable presence of mind he rushed to the anti-parachutist alarm and sounded it, whereupon everybody put on their gas masks. The final report on the state of preparedness in the Headquarters was tactfully shelved.

Early in September I was detailed to go and meet a liaison officer of high rank on his way from the War Office to General

Wavell's Headquarters in Cairo. He was due to arrive by 'plane that morning and as his Wellington was circling over the aerodrome the air raid alert sounded. We were standing by the side of his 'plane when the local alarm for Luqa aerodrome went off and as he heard it he turned to me and said "Do you ever get bombed here?" I suppressed a faint smile and murmured, "Just occasionally".

"Well you can't have any idea of what we have been having in London. The bombing is simply frightful and the barrage is almost worse. No one can get a wink of sleep and conditions are such that you can have no conception of them out here".

I expressed my sympathy suitably and enquired where he was in all this holocaust.

"Oh, well, I actually am in a tube station," he replied, "but the noise is so frightful that you can't get a wink of sleep."

At that moment we saw the bombers approaching and I said to him: "It looks like an attack on Luqa. We had better jump into this ditch" which was a small slit trench that a Maltese workman had prudently dug for himself before commencing work.

On came the bombers with anti-aircraft fire seemingly very accurate all round them. Suddenly one dropped and then another and then another followed by another. It was too good to be true. People on the aerodrome were shouting excitedly that we were shooting them all down. However, opinions changed as from the leader came a clutch of bombs. This was the first and only dive bombing attack ever to be made by the Italians on Malta. They used JU87s with Italian markings and christened them Picchiatelli in honour of the change. The bombing was remarkably good. They hit practically every hangar and also scored a direct hit on the Wellington in which this officer had so lately arrived. We were not very far from that and when the attack was over we scrambled out of the trench and this officer, wiping his face, said: "I think General Wavell would like me to get along as soon as I can." And this time I fear I smiled a little more obviously.

While he was having breakfast I wandered round the aerodrome having a look at the damage, in company with a Fleet Air Arm Pilot. Approaching his office, which appeared to have been slightly hit, we strolled in somewhat unconcernedly but our speed in retreat was unrivalled as the first thing we saw was a whacking great bomb leaning up against his safe. I am sure we did more damage to the remaining hangers in our headlong flight than the bombing itself had done.

Later that evening I had the unusual experience of interviewing and cross-examining one of the Italian pilots who had escorted the bombers on their mission. We got a lot of interesting facts about our Anti-aircraft out of him and he expressed a healthy respect for it, which was natural as we had shot him down. I then told him that I was lucky to be there questioning him, whereupon he said: "Now give me what you English call 'fair-dos'. Was our bombing good?"

This particular officer was a fanatical Fascist and he was very cheerful about being taken prisoner, merely remarking that it was the fortune of war and we would all be his prisoners within a month. Before he left the Island he became rapidly anti-Mussolini as he had been given every opportunity of listening in to the Italian news broadcasts and propaganda and comparing it with what he actually saw with his own eyes.

Mention of the Fleet Air Arm pilot makes me think of that gallant band of Swordfish pilots who night after night, whenever the moon was suitable, would go out in their old crates attacking heavily escorted Axis convoys on their way to Libya. Frankie Howie, whom I had known in Hong Kong, was their leader and he must have been a tremendous source of inspiration to them all. When France fell he flew his flight (with motor cycles attached to the wings and every conceivable form of overloading of stores and personal equipment) from France to Tunisia where he was certain he would find the French prepared to carry on the struggle. On arrival there he at once sensed the atmosphere of doubt and hesitancy and immediately packed up again and brought his gallant band to Malta where they were to play such a vital part for so long in the offensive operations launched against the Axis shipping. His reward of the DSO was earned not once but again and again. There was one famous story told of him when he was about to attack a convoy which was just entering Tripoli harbour. Flak was pouring up on all sides and his companion in the 'plane asked him for instructions as to what to do. With shells bursting and searchlights piercing the sky all round him Frankie was to be seen studying a map and saying, "I can't quite make out where we are". The soldiers in the coast defence forts near Hal Far, from which he operated used to give those Swordfish crews some very hearty cheers as they sped out into the growing twilight on their missions.

It may be advisable here to try and give some kind of picture of the life that everyone was leading in this front line outpost. To be perfectly truthful, it was not very different from normal. Still no mails arrived and so there were no home papers, but food and drink were to be had in plenty provided you could get to them—transport was very scarce. Dances were held once a week at the Club; women wore their evening dresses and many officers changed into their "blues" at night.

Although distances are short in Malta, the roads are very bad and facilities for transport were definitely cut down, and so it became difficult to meet friends very often. So in September, to celebrate my birthday, I decided to throw a cocktail party in my flat. It started off as all such parties do in a very respectable atmosphere with everybody very glad to meet each other again, not having seen them since the day before. It ended with a note of hilarity in the middle of an air-raid, which drew down upon us the wrath of one irate officer who apparently considered that Italian pilots would hear the noise we were making and that their notorious inaccuracy of aim might cause them to hit his house instead of the one we were occupying.

However, half way through the party, which contained a large element of the erstwhile theatrical set, an idea was born which subsequently bore much fruit. At the time that it was decided to produce "French Without Tears" a play by Philip Johnson called "Lovers' Leap" had also been actively canvassed as an alternative. I had seen it in London and thought it a very witty and beautifully acted comedy. Nora Swinburne and Ursula Jeans played the leading roles with Owen Nares and Walter Hudd in the London production. A cast of four and a butler were all that was required.

Everybody was keen to try and get some entertainment going for the benefit of officers and troops alike, but the MADC had always produced at the Opera House and that was now taken over for ARP purposes. Besides, the difficulties of collecting any cast and arranging rehearsals seemed to put a full-length play out of consideration for production. Suddenly I said to Kay Warren "Why not do a series of plays with small casts such as 'Lovers' Leap' and use our tiny Club stage? It would be much more fun to give a number of performances to small audiences as the hall only seats seventy, than to spend months rehearsing and polishing a play just for the sake of one or two performances in the vast acreage of the Opera House". Kay Warren immediately began turning the idea over in her mind and I meanwhile walked over to Philip Calderon and got him interested in it too. With Kay, Philip and myself all willing to act we already had three-quarters of the cast and it only remained to find the ingenue, and she luckily was present at the party in the person of Patricia Coghill. Tall, blonde and extremely easy to look upon, she became all enthusiasm and immediately took charge of the three of us, practically forcing us to read the play there and then.

Well, there were many difficulties to be faced. Scarcity of transport, the possibility of raids and last, but not least, the difficulties of ever synchronising our hours off duty. But still the idea grew and in a very short time the cast of four principles was actively rehearsing, and only the character of Poynter, the butler, remained to be filled.

There were various scenic effects such as the thunder storm and lightning that had to be achieved on a stage not much larger than a couple of tables put together, and with only eighteen inches between the back cloth and the outside wall. To add to the difficulties there was only one dressing room into which all the props had to be stored as well, and altogether it seemed an almost insuperable feat to produce realistic thunder and drenching rain. However, we had counted without the resources of the Royal Navy and like a gift from heaven Peter Bartlett appeared in command of one of His Majesty's submarines. She was to be docked for repairs and so we knew we were sure of him for a few weeks. With masterly efficiency he tackled not only the stage effects for which he raided the dockyard and any other Government department that he thought might be useful, but he also became stage manager. Finally he also stepped with the utmost dignity into the part of Poynter, earning on the occasion of the first performance a round of applause all to himself for a bit of "business" that he had put in originally on the spur of the moment one day at rehearsal when one of the members of the cast failed to squeeze along behind the back cloth in time to make an entrance on the cue.

The play was produced in November and ran for eight matinees. Philip Calderon played Owen Nares part, Kay Warren turned in a magnificent performance as his wife, Patricia Coghill feasted the eye in Ursula Jeans' role and I played the part of Cedric Norreys, her repressed and nervous suitor. We did not have a single seat vacant for any of the performances and I would not like to say how many we crammed in for the last one. Our expenses had been little and we managed to make a considerable amount of money, some of which went to Malta charities while the remainder was used as a nest egg to finance future productions.

If one is going to attempt to give a true picture of four years of life it is idle to pretend that every path was strewn with roses or that setbacks and disappointments did not occur. The rough must be taken with the smooth and obstacles are there to be surmounted. Maybe in the end one is all the better for

Patricia Coghill and the author in a scene from
the MADC production of "Lovers' Leap".
December 1940.

having faced up to them but it is difficult to believe it at the time. Less than an hour before the opening performance of "Lovers' Leap" a knock came on the door of our combined dressing-cum-green room as we were making up and the odour of Leichner No. 9 and No. 5 was filling the air. This necessitated a hurried scurrying behind the screen by Pat Coghill and Kay Warren who, to put it mildly, were attired only in scanties. A kind and thoughtful soldier from my office appeared: "Mail just in, Sir; and there's a letter for you." I thanked him profusely while the others just looked on with envy. Only those who have experienced months of anxiety without news from home, apart from greatly delayed cables, can realise what the arrival of letters can mean. Here at last was news—detailed news—of all the hard times they had been enduring in England under the onslaught from the air, and the threat of invasion. There was time to read it before putting on the final touches of make-up and eagerly I tore the envelope open. But alas, this eagerly awaited letter was to be the fore-runner of very great personal sadness and anxiety which was to continue throughout the months and years that followed. Even in the midst of all her pre-occupations with making-up, props, lighting and a last minute revision of her cues, Kay found time to notice my distress. It was only through her that I was able to play the comedy role of Cedric Norreys at that first perform-ance. With her aid we locked the spectre in a back cupboard of the mind for three hours. After that the safety valve could lift and it did.

On the completion of our run in the Club rooms we took "Lovers' Leap" out to several locations so that more troops could see it. It had meant weeks of hard work in the only spare time that we had, but it had all been so very well worth-while.

Just before the production was due to take place a new GSO1 arrived in the person of Colonel Bill Bedford. Bill, although I was not to know it at the time, was to be one of my best friends and he immediately became interested when he heard of our efforts, promising to attend the second performance. He was the possessor of perhaps the loudest voice I have ever heard in any man and from the moment that he first guffawed that performance was made as he proceeded to laugh for the remaining two and a half hours, and to laugh so loudly and so long that we had to hold up our lines for what seemed hours in order that those at the back of the hall could hear them. Poor Bill, I wish his laughter could still be heard in this world. Alas, after filling a very difficult job in Malta he went home to take command of a Regiment of the Ayrshire Yeomanry and was killed leading them into action in North Africa just before the battle was won.

I retired to hospital just before Christmas day with a mild attack of influenza. This was my only experience of hospital in Malta and let me say here and now that the medical authorities performed wonders out there and we were extremely fortunate to have such excellent doctors and nurses. However, military hospital is no place to spend Christmas with all its insistence on straight bedspreads and other military necessities of life—and death—with the result that I perpetrated this libel entitled "Abandon Hope All Ye Who Enter Here". The hospital authorities I am glad to say took no offence and even printed it (without my permission) in the next issue of their monthly magazine. The absence of doctors that is noted in the rhyme was due to a series of hockey matches in which game the RAMC excelled.

ABANDON HOPE ALL YE WHO ENTER HERE

When you're feeling rather seedy and you think you
        want to die,
    I can tell you just exactly where to go;
There's a Military Hospital, eight hundred feet up
        high,
    With a cemetery all handy just below.
They've a staff of charming nurses to set your bed just
        right,
    And Orderlies quite deaf to all you say,
There's a padre to administer your last religious rite,
    And "Fly Control's" the order of the day.
Everything is ready for your wish to be fulfilled,
    In fact before they ever let you in
They insist that every detail on a special form is filled
    Of your religion and your nearest next of kin.
You mustn't take your pistol or bring along your
        towels,
    To do either seems unpardonable sin.
Soon a somewhat harrassed sister will enquire about
        your bowels
    And tuck the bedclothes tightly round your chin.
Your temperature taken and your pulse rate noted
        down,
    There is nothing left to do but lie and wait
'Til yet another sister with a rather angry frown
    Reprimands you 'cos your bed-spread isn't
        straight.

If your bed is at an angle of five or ten degrees
    They may go and make a faulty diagnosis,
For it's probably a symptom to be recognised with ease
    That the patient has acute tuberculosis.
For the ordinary sick who may wish to live again,
    I'm told they keep a sanitary squad,
But for rather graver cases and those who are in pain
    They leave it all to Nature and to God.
There is one thing I must tell you and you must really
    get it clear,
    I should hate to cause you any shattered hopes,
You'll NEVER see a doctor for as long as you are
    there
    In spite of all your specimens and dopes.
The last time one was seen was on a Christmas Eve,
    An expiring patient said: "At last, at last,
I know it's much too late, but a doctor I perceive,
    The age of miracles is surely never past."

And so 1940 drew to its close. It had certainly been an eventful year. The phoney war in Europe had suddenly changed into the Blitzkrieg in a form and strength that had never been anticipated. France battered from without and rotten within crashed to her fall. Malta, alone in the middle of the Mediterranean, became an easy prey for the Fascist Dictator, but the seemingly inevitable had not happened. Malta still stood and defied all the Italian efforts to subdue her by bombing. The life of the people was almost normal; offensive operations both under the sea and in the air took place regularly from its shores; General Wavell's army was hurling the Italians in headlong flight along the Libyan coast and the situation appeared rosy indeed for the Island of the Knights. But 1941 was to dawn and with it came the Germans with their screaming Stukas and their Messerschmitts bringing a new conception of what aerial warfare could mean. But that is a development which belongs to the next scene.

CHAPTER V

The Plot Develops

THE first few days of the New Year gave no portent of what was to come. It was almost common knowledge that a convoy was expected, not because of any lack of Naval security, but because of the uncanny habit the Maltese had of always knowing, seemingly weeks in advance, when the next lot of ships could be expected. At the end of the first week it was established that two convoys were due to arrive—one from Alexandria and one from the West. But the arrival of convoys so far had caused no great heightening of the scale of attack by our Italian enemies.

One morning there came down the ramp of Lascaris Barracks a very small officer in a red hat accompanied by rather a tall Captain. It appeared that he had come all the way out from England via South Africa to assume the post of AADC Malta, which was already filled by someone else. As it was not easy either to get to, or away from, Malta, there was rather naturally a flutter in the dovecotes when this complication came to light. However, it transpired that the new arrival had been in charge of the Dover AA defences during the Battle of Britain. Not only that, but his guns had shot down some ninety 'planes themselves, and he had been awarded the OBE for his gallantry and unremitting good work during those testing days. An AA Bde was in process of formation but the selection of the commander was still unsettled so this arrival actually came like a gift from Heaven, and Brigadier Sadler assumed command of the Seventh AA Brigade.

Two days later, to my great surprise, Bill Bedford told me that I was to leave him and go as Brigade Major to the new Brigadier. He added: "I must give you a word of warning. He doesn't want you in the least as he has brought out his own officer and is very disgruntled that he can't have him for Brigade Major." I was led out to meet this Brigadier and had a very uncomfortable ten minutes making myself known to him whilst the two of us were overlooked by the imposing presence of the officer whom unwittingly I had supplanted. Brigadier Sadler said later that when he was told that his Brigade Major was going to be selected for him he immediately took a poor view of any officer that might be chosen, but took an even poorer one when he was informed that his new Brigade Major knew nothing about AA Artillery, but acted in plays and was acquainted with everyone in Malta. It was not until a few days later that I was able to take up the appointment with him, but from the very beginning we worked in the closest harmony and I could never hope to serve a nicer or more gallant commander.

Shortly after this the other convoy arrived in Malta having taken a pasting en route and with its chief escort vessel, HMS Illustrious badly damaged as a result of four concentrated attacks by German Stukas. "Illustrious" limped into French Creek in Malta's Grand Harbour and tied up to effect quick repairs.

Almost immediately Brigadier Sadler sensed the danger in which Malta lay. He had had experience of dive bombing from his days at Dover. He enquired at once whether there was a box barrage designed to cover the Grand Harbour. Now Malta had only had one dive bombing attack, which I have already related, and as a result the question of defensive measures against their tactics had not been exhaustively discussed. Brigadier Sadler took a strong line and made it clear that he would not accept the responsibility for the defence of HMS Illustrious if a box barrage was not immediately devised for her protection. Everyone was naturally anxious that he should assume that responsibility and so orders were got out for the preparation of the barrage. Officers worked desperately into the small hours of the morning plotting co-ordinates and sending out orders to guns to ensure that the whole of the area over French Creek would be suitably covered by shell bursts in the event of a concentrated attack, and that no gaps should be left through which the Stukas might bomb with comparative immunity. On the 16th January at about a quarter past twelve, a special announcement was broadcast over the Island's wireless rediffusion system that in the event of an air raid civilian personnel must take cover as new tactics were going to be employed by the AA Artillery. At 1355 hours, after a preliminary reconnaissance by one 'plane, the attack came in force. The radar plot was the largest that had ever been recorded in Malta till then and there was no doubt that the Germans were going to make a determined effort to cripple the "Illustrious"; but how determined that effort was going to be no one could have had

Jan 1941. The attack on HMS Illustrious, which can be discerned lying under the crane.

any idea until they saw it in practice. I stood with General Scobell, the GOC, and several other officers in a window casement for the first attack. Out of the sun came wave after wave of JU-87s and JU-88s. Malta's barrage roared up in earnest for the first time and over seventy enemy bombers braved its might. They were heavily escorted by fighters and so the four Hurricanes and three Fulmars which were all that Malta's defences could provide, decided to lie off the coast and make sure of killing the lame ducks as they came away from that hail of lead.

It seemed impossible that anything could survive the holocaust of bombs that fell around that ship. The German pilots dived with the greatest gallantry almost to point blank range. They secured one hit in the Captain's cabin, but otherwise the "Illustrious" escaped this attack unscathed. Lying on the opposite side of the Creek to the "Illustrious" was a merchant ship, the "Essex" which was crammed with thousands of tons of explosives. A heavy armour-piercing bomb dropped directly on this ship and penetrated right into the engine room. Parts of the ship blew miles into the air, but by a miracle the ammunition failed to explode. Had it done so few of us who were in that area would be alive to tell the tale.

During the second phase of the attack I went out to a light AA position overlooking French Creek and there I saw a JU-87 dive right though that curtain of steel, release his bomb almost at the last moment and then turn and fly only a few feet above the water down French Creek and turn right handed towards the entrance to the harbour. He was so low that he had to rise to clear the Mole at the harbour mouth. A Fulmar pilot followed him throughout the whole of his course regardless not only of the heavy AA barrage, but also of the enormous concentration of tracer shells from the Bofors guns and from "Illustrious" herself. As the Stuka rose to clear the Mole he shot him into the sea on the far side and then landed at Hal Far, remarking that he "did not think much of Malta's bloody barrage." He confessed later that he never flew that 'plane again and how he ever landed it was a mystery, so badly was it knocked about.

The noise of the barrage was stupendous and the whole Island literally bounced under the impact of such a heavy concentration of bombs. One could feel the ground tremble under one's feet about a second after every big bomb entered the water and as each salvo of guns was fired. HMS Illustrious herself struck me at that moment as being rather like a great cat at bay. She had her back arched up against the walls of the cliffs rising sheer from the docks and her guns were spitting back defiance at any and every target that came within range. It was a magnificent sight—something that can never be described adequately on paper and the bravery of the crew and of the men, both British and Maltese, of the Light AA guns all round her was only equalled by that of the German pilots who faced that avalanche of death unflinchingly.

At the height of this pandemonium a Maltese friend of mine, Harry Micallief, with whom I had been at the young officers course at Larkhill some ten years before, was celebrating his marriage. It certainly was a stormy beginning to what has since proved a very happy alliance.

The Germans took a bad knock on this first attack and next day they left Malta severely alone, but on the 18th they returned again with even more 'planes. Everybody braced themselves for another attack on the "Illustrious", but this time they went for Luqa aerodrome and tried to knock out Malta's fighter effort. But again Brigadier Sadler had thought ahead of them. He had realised that this might be their next tactic and he had ordered barrages to be prepared to cover both Luqa and Hal Far aerodromes. The Germans attacked Luqa as bravely as they had attacked the "Illustrious", but they suffered even heavier losses at the hands of Malta's fighters and AA defences.

The following day they made two more attacks on "Illustrious" (both in the morning), and they lost eighteen 'planes in the two attacks. It was evident that either the Second Eleven was bowling that day or else they realised at last the strength of the AA and fighter defences that they had to face. There was not the same determination in the pressing home of the attack, but even so the "Illustrious" sustained one more hit.

It might be of interest to note that in the last attack almost 3,400 rounds of heavy AA ammunition and over 4,000 rounds of light AA ammunition were expended by the ground defences alone, quite apart from the "Illustrious" own contribution to her defence.

These hits on the aircraft carrier had made it questionable whether she would ever be able to get away. In case it was found impossible plans were discussed for removing her armament of 4.5 inch AA guns and mounting them for Malta's defence as it seemed impossible that she could continue to weather the fury of the Nazi storm. But the miracle happened. The German Air Force under Field Marshal Kesselring had had enough. In those attacks they had lost forty 'planes for sure and rumours reached us later of mass burials in Sicily of members of the crews of those which managed to struggle back to their base. Their losses were too severe and they gave the "Illustrious" the breathing space necessary to effect quick repairs.

Three days later with our hearts in our mouths we watched her cast off from the quay side and nose her way out towards Elmo lighthouse. Just as she was coming abreast the harbour entrance the air alarm went. It seemed that the Germans must have known of her departure and were only waiting until she was out of effective range of the Island's AA artillery before they launched their final coup de grace on the stricken ship. The suspense was tremendous. But either the reconnaissance 'plane failed to spot her or else it was a stray German 'plane that had flown out of its course. No attack materialised and HMS Illustrious made her way at twenty-three knots through the hours of darkness to safety in Alexandria.

Malta had certainly felt the full fury of the onslaught. The three cities which comprise the area surrounding the harbour were devastated. The beautiful little chapel of St. Angelo fort was destroyed and the scene in the dock yard was one of utter devastation. But yet it had been worth it and the Prime Minister's words in the House of Commons in praise of Malta's spirit and defence put great heart into the whole Island and made them resolved to face the worst that Kesselring could do with his fleets of aircraft based only sixty miles away.

During these raids Brigadier Sadler rapidly earned the affection and admiration of all the soldiery under his command. By reason of his small stature he was immediately christened either "Gordon Richards" or "Pocket Battleship" and this last name was the one that stuck to him for the rest of his time in Malta. Wherever the bombs were falling thickest there he was to be seen and his fury when he and I missed a later raid on Hal Far aerodrome while out on a reconnaissance for new gun positions was as unbounded as was my relief. He seemed to know no fear at all and the soldiers used to tell me what it meant to them to see his stocky little figure in a very large tin hat striding into the gun pit at the height of the attack.

After the escape of "Illustrious" the Luftwaffe paused to lick its wounds and for some time we were spared the heavy raids such as we had experienced during those hectic days, but instead were treated to long night visitations by Italian bombers. However, at the end of February they made another attack in strength on Luqa aerodrome, again suffered heavy losses and

Pat Coghill as Helen Hayle and the author as The Duke of
Bristol in "On Approval".   Malta 1941.

had to stop very large scale raids until March 5th when they made a concentrated assault on the aerodrome at Hal Far. JU-87s, JU-88s and Dorniers, heavily escorted by fighters, took part in this attack. It cost them fifteen 'planes, but apart from damage to buildings, Hal Far aerodrome only suffered a final loss of one Swordfish and one member of the Devon Regiment who was incapacitated by a splinter in his knee. The clouds of dust and the noise of the explosions and the barrage made it impossible to believe that anything could survive in the area of that aerodrome and one was not surprised when one listened to the glowing accounts on the German wireless of the results of their attack. If only they could have known the real outcome of their efforts they would have been very disappointed men.

Another convoy arrived in March and the Germans proceeded to attack it, but by now they were very wary of how they approached Malta's vulnerable points. There was little determination to press home the bombing and the whole convoy escaped unscathed allowing more AA reinforcements to land in Malta.

Their crippling losses in these big day attacks now caused the Germans to alter their tactics in exactly the same way as they had done in the Battle of Britain. Night raiding in force, with the whole Island lit up by thousands of flares, became their primary method of attack. Day raids still continued but with small numbers of bombers bombing from comparatively high levels. But each night was indeed a trial to the inhabitants of Malta. HMS Gloucester and a flotilla of destroyers under the command of Captain Lord Louis Mountbatten had lately based themselves on Malta and were carrying out highly successful raids against Axis shipping. This was a target well worth the air effort which the Germans expended against it, but in spite of parachute mines and bombs of every calibre, not one of those ships was hit while under the protection of Malta's defences.

During the quiet intervals between raids, Philip Calderon, Kay Warren, Pat Coghill and myself had again been hatching a production for the entertainment of Malta. We had decided to repeat the experiment of "Lovers' Leap" and to produce a similar kind of play, Frederick Lonsdale's "On Approval". As can well be imagined, rehearsals for this were even more difficult to arrange, or to survive, than they had been for "Lovers' Leap", but we were determined that nothing should stand in our way. And so throughout the last fortnight in March and the month of April, we learnt our parts and rehearsed our scenes in the quiet intervals between the raids. Lord Louis Mountbatten whose flotilla was based on Malta at this time, was delighted to find that the Malta Amateur Dramatic Club, of which he had been a member in the past, was struggling to produce theatrical entertainment in the face of all these difficulties and he attended several of the rehearsals.

This time we were without the able help of Peter Bartlett and we had to do all the stage management and scene shifting ourselves. I often wondered if those audiences who saw Kay Warren play Mrs. Wislack so well could have pictured her, just a few hours before, arranging the seats, briefing the door keeper, struggling with fuses, hauling stage furniture about, and in fact working herself to a stand still, ably assisted by Pat Coghill. These two did all the dirty work in preparation for every performance whilst Philip Calderon and I worked to the last moment in our offices before rushing to change and make-up, often uncertain whether we should be able to get away in time for the actual performance.

In the middle of these rehearsals in April I had a succession of narrow escapes from bombing which left me in no fit state to cope with the onerous part of the Duke of Bristol and still less with the duties of Brigade Major. So for three days I took a break in the neighbouring Island of Gozo, and occupied myself in writing the first draft of a play that in final form much interested that fascinating and delightful actress Ann Todd. With her encouragement it may yet see the light of day. Three times within a week I had been on gun sites which had received direct hits and on the only night on which I had decided to have a dinner in comfort at the Club, rather than going out to the draughty light AA position overlooking the Harbour which was our usual stand, a parachute mine fell in the middle of the Valetta main street. It proceeded to wreck the dining room where I was trying to shut the blackout shutters which had been blown open by a small bomb a few moments before. I had the luck to escape with only a few scratches and cuts but a naval officer who helped me was blown right on to the "cold table".

It was nice to go to Gozo and to hear the air raid warning wailing and to feel that one would not have to duck at any moment. Contentedly I rolled over in my bed as I saw the searchlights light up, and merely hoped that all my friends would escape unscathed. My reverie was rudely disturbed by the familiar whistle developing into a shriek and a loud explosion less than one hundred yards away from the hotel. Some German bomber had mistaken Gozo for Malta, or else had dropped his bombs early before he met the Malta night defences.

Mention of these defences makes me think of George Bell, who had come out as the Battery Commander of a heavy AA Territorial Battery, bringing with him as Battery Captain, Nick Harrison, who was to be a tower of strength, not only to me personally, but also the whole of Malta. Nick's great girth and even greater bonhomie were only matched by his personal courage and determination to see everything from the receiving end in order that he could help with suggestions for defeating the bombers. He and I worked together for nearly two years in the closest harmony and together we contrived to retain our senses of humour even when things looked blackest.

George Bell worked out in conjunction with Captain Appleby of the REs, a brilliant mathematician, a vast series of co-ordinates in the sky. Even now I boggle at the thought of the scope of the task they performed. The details of the scheme are too complicated to explain in this book, but suffice it to say that all the guns of the Island could be brought to fire on any point in the sky at the same moment. In order to ensure that an aircraft was at that particular point in the sky at the moment when the shells of the defences would burst, one had, however, to know the height of the 'plane. George and I dined night after night in the Union Club trying to work out some solution to this problem, but until the arrival of the necessary type of instrument we were never able to get nearer than a wild guess based upon a mixture of chianti, George's judgement of Italian pilots and his thirteen years experience as a child in Italy. With these as a basis and with Henry Heath, our instructor in fire control, to help work out the technical detail, we shot our barrage into the sky. Not many 'planes were destroyed by them, as can well be imagined, but the Island was saved an immense tonnage of bombs being dropped on it by the fact that we discovered that the Italian bombers would drop their bombs as soon as they saw the flashes of the guns. It was not long, therefore, before we decided to open fire on them when they were still out of range and, in consequence, the majority of Italian bombs fell harmlessly into the sea. When the Germans came to the attack, however, our methods were obviously too bow-and-arrow but the large number of shell bursts in the sky and the blinding tactics of the searchlights contrived to make the German bombing very inaccurate until they came low, when the Bofors and small arms were able to engage them to good effect.

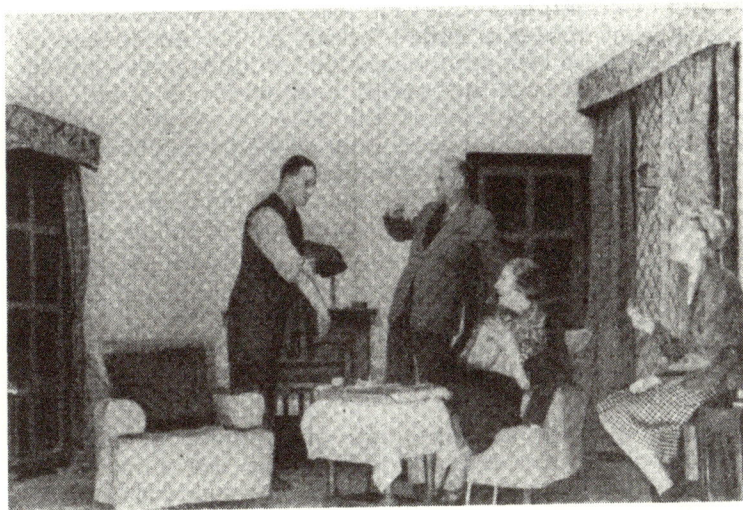

A scene from "On Approval" showing Kay Warren as Mrs Wislack, Patricia Coghill as Helen Hayle, Philip Calderon as Richard, and the author as The Duke of Bristol. May 1941.

Early in May night raiding suddenly ceased and even day raiding was confined to ME-109s scattering bombs at random over the Island. It seemed that the Luftwaffe had called the battle off. We in Malta, of course, were not to know that this was in preparation for the onslaught on Crete and later the fatal attack on Russia.

During their attacks the Axis had lost one hundred and fifteen 'planes for certain and thirty five which almost certainly could never have got back to their bases. What they had achieved was little in the way of material damage to Malta's war effort. They had not prevented the submarines sailing or the gallant sorties by Swordfish or the harassing of their shipping lines by cruisers and destroyers. They had prevented any large scale reinforcement of Malta's fighters, but the AA defences of the Island had been increased and the few fighters that remained in Malta, although out gunned and inferior in speed, still managed to take their toll of Axis raiders by day and by night. Damage to civilian populated areas of Valetta and Sliema and to the cities surrounding the harbours had been very considerable and in some cases quite wanton. All in all it was a poor return for the loss of so many 'planes and skilled air crews.

Nevertheless the respite was welcome. Gaily we accepted the situation and turned our thoughts to lighter things. At the end of May during a spell of particularly hot weather the four members of the MADC production of "On Approval" proceeded to put on their overcoats and their scarves and to pretend that it was snowing in Scotland.

It is always difficult to write of something in which one has been actively concerned such as this play in which not only did I have the chance to play the unprincipled Duke, but also to collaborate, as in the case of "Lovers' Leap", with Kay Warren in its production. But the applause that greeted every performance justifies me in saying that it was no whit less successful than its predecessor. In fact we played more performances and never was there a vacant seat in the house. Patricia Coghill with her hair swept up in little clusters of curls on the top of her head looked a picture of loveliness and handled to perfection the scene where she refuses His Grace. Philip Calderon won everyone's sympathy as the hapless Richard, while Kay Warren became Mrs. Wislack to the life. So well did she play that I found myself almost hating her in reality at the end of every performance. If it had not been for the fact that as soon as the curtain was down between scenes the lazy selfish Duke and the tyrannical Wislack had to drop their roles and hectically help the others to change the props the illusion would have been complete. When we went on tour it seemed to go down with the troops even better than "Lovers' Leap" although as a cast I believe we all felt happier in the former play.

I gave a luncheon party before the opening performance at which a new RAF arrival attended—W/Cdr Grant-Ferris the MP for Paddington. He said at the time, when thanking me for the lunch and for the performance, that he hoped he would repay it in the near future. I had almost forgotten what he had said until in March, 1944 I attended a sumptuous dinner at the Savoy which he and his charming wife gave to reunite some of the veterans of Malta's darker days.

Also present at this dinner were two people with whom I first came into close contact just before "On Approval" was produced. One was Peter Read-Davies who in his various capacities as Camouflage Officer and then as GSO3(I) did noble work for Malta, and whose house, which for a long time he shared with Bill Bedford, was the acme of hospitality, good taste and escapism from the hard realities of war. Peter was not new to stage productions as he had been intimately concerned in the production of at least two successful London Revues. He was an artist at design and the sets that he produced for "On Approval" won universal admiration. On such a tiny stage it is very difficult to give any impression of space but somehow Peter contrived, by the modernity and lightness of his touch, to convey the impression, first of a full-sized London drawing room and then of a Scottish baronial hall. His ingenuity was unlimited; at the very last moment we thought that a picture must be hung in a certain space in order to cover a gap on the back cloth. Within half an hour Peter had produced an extremely modernistic drawing on a mirror which, although it appeared on close inspection to bear little resemblance to any living thing, yet at a distance and across the foot-lights exactly hit off and absorbed the whole spirit of his decor.

The other personage present at this dinner party at the Savoy carried more guns both literally and figuratively. He was Major-General C. T. Beckett who was CRA of Malta from May 1941 right through the times of stress and danger until Christmas 1942 when he was able to leave the Island conscious of a magnificent job magnificently done. I was privileged to work with him for all but two months of his time in Malta and my admiration of all that he did during his tenure of office will never diminish. Rather will it increase as the years lend a proper perspective to the decisions and measures that he had to take and the responsibility he shouldered.

Towards the end of May 1941 Brigadier Beckett, as he was then, was appointed CRA Malta, and arrived in company with AVM H. P. Lloyd who had just been appointed AOC of the Island. The two of them attended the second performance of "On Approval" and certainly seemed to appreciate the humour of the play as both were extremely complimentary later about our performances. I still had a feeling, however, that the new CRA was wondering how it was possible to fit in theatricals with the stern business of war. I was right too, because he queried Brigadier Sadler on the point, but the Brigadier satisfied him that I had only utilised the hours of recreation and rest for this purpose. The fact that we were providing entertainment for the Island which was largely devoid of such relaxation obviously appealed to him as he realised from the first the importance of recreation for all ranks and encouraged every effort to provide it.

One of the first results of his arrival in Malta was the transfer of our Brigade HQ out to St. Julian's Bay. After much fierce opposition from my Brigadier who had his eye on one abandoned gun position, we took over the lovely house formerly occupied by the previous AOC and very soon had it all luxuriously fitted up and appointed. This was entirely in accordance with the CRA's principles that any one could make himself uncomfortable—a favourite dictum of his.

It was while we were out there that very early one morning I heard the "All Clear" go after a short night raid to be followed some ten minutes later by a colossal explosion somewhere in the harbour area. Almost at the same moment there was a lot of Bofors and small arms fire and then suddenly the clatter was increased by the barking of other high velocity guns. This appeared to be no ordinary air raid and I rushed up to the roof in my pyjamas in company with the rest of the HQ to see what was afoot. A fantastic sight met our eyes. Bofors were sending out red balls of fire which were bouncing off the sea and searchlights were sweeping across the harbour mouths. Green streaks of light from the twin six pounders of the coastal defences were intermingling with the Bofors tracer and darting up and down in the most fantastic curves.

It was thrilling to watch, but none of us were fully aware of what was happening. The firing died down and we were able to get a call through to the harbour Fire Commander who told us that an attack by Italian "E" boats on the convoy that had just got in had taken place and that one torpedo had struck somewhere on the foreshore without doing any appreciable damage.

The CRA Malta and his principal officers. Of those mentioned in the text of the book the following can be discerned:— Front row (left to right) Lt-Col Clark (Chief Instructor in Gunnery, Malta); Brig Sadler (Cmdr LAA Bde); Brig Gatt (Col Comdt); Maj-Gen Beckett; Brig Hire (Cmdr HAA Bde); Brig C. J. White (Cmdr Fixed Defences); and Col Woolley. On either side of the CRA in the second row are the author and Nick Harrison.

At that moment the firing broke out anew, and this time redoubled in intensity as everyone warmed to their work. At the height of it the sky began to turn a delicate pink in the East. Dawn was approaching and with it Hurricane fighters took off and flew low over the harbour approaches, adding their contribution to the general confusion and clamour of the hour.

The Italians had planned the attack extremely carefully. If all had gone well their "E" boats and one-man submarines were to leave their parent ship some distance away from Malta and to creep towards the harbour synchronising their approach to the entrance with an aerial bombardment. As so often happened, however, the Italian Air Force let their comrades down as not only was their attack over before the small vessels got into position, but it was completely ineffective with all the bombs dropping harmlessly into the sea. Otherwise it is possible that the initial torpedo which struck against a stanchion of a bridge jutting out to the harbour mole might have been mistaken for a bomb and so facilitated entrance to the harbour and aided the possible destruction of the valuable merchant ships. As it was this well aimed blow occurred after the "All Clear" had sounded and, in addition, struck in such a way that the passage between the mole and the foreshore was made even more difficult because, instead of submarine chains and a boom obstructing the way, the actual solid structure of the bridge collapsed into the water. However, even before that shot had been fired, the lookouts had observed the approach of the "E" boats and the firing had commenced. When one remembers that night after night for years now the coastal gunners had been in a high state of readiness with their lookouts constantly on the alert for the approach of any small craft without a sign of enemy action occurring, it is a great tribute to their keeness that they seized the opportunity with such eagerness and skill. The defensive tactics have been cited as a model of coast artillery practice and the results were satisfactory in the extreme. Seventeen small craft left the parent ship to wreak destruction on the convoy that had sailed unmolested through the Mediterranean and seventeen small craft failed to return. For months the Italian press continued to glorify the triumphant exploits of the brave men who manned these infernal machines, but the fantastic claims they made for ships sunk in the attack showed that they had no knowledge of what really had transpired and later they admitted, and it was confirmed through the reports of prisoners of war, that the attack had been a one hundred percent failure. The action was a particular triumph for the Maltese as not only were they manning the coastal guns of the harbour but it was their LAA Regiment which was in that area, too.

Only two days after this attack the CRA carried out an inspection of our Brigade area. I had seen him after lunch in the Club the day before and we had had a very pleasant ten minutes talk. On the day of the inspection I was very anxious for Brigadier Sadler to get the CRA's approval for some project that we planned. I have forgotten what it was now, but I remember we were doubtful whether he would agree to it. In actual fact he agreed to more than we anticipated and he smilingly said to me: "Will that do you?" When I replied: "Well it is the thin end of the wedge, thank you very much, Sir", he startled me by saying "You had better come and see about the rest of the wedge from my office as I want you to join my staff in a few days time." This shook me considerably as I felt sure that I was in no way qualified to act as chief staff officer, without the benefit of clergy at Haifa or Camberley, on matters that had to be settled at so high a level as HQ Royal Artillery Malta. Already there had been many changes in the constitution of that staff and so it was with considerable trepidation I transferred myself to Brigadier Beckett's Headquarters a few mornings later. This nervousness was greatly increased by Bill Bedford asking me what I was doing there. Quickly and thoughtlessly I replied, "Oh, I've joined the In-and-Out." Whereupon he went straight into the CRA and related the story. I am glad to say, however, that Joe Beckett, as he is universally known in the Army as was his brother in the Navy, has a prodigious and brilliant sense of humour which varies from topical and timely allusions to the Scriptures to Rabelaisian wit of the deepest dye, and he appeared to be delighted at this story. It may well have proved the cornerstone of the happy relations that I had with him for the rest of his time in Malta. At any rate he suggested christening his room "No. 94".

CHAPTER VI

Interval

It was now the beginning of August 1941 and Malta had experienced fourteen months of actual hostilities against the Axis. Maybe it is time just for a short while to take stock of what had happened and how the resistance of the Island had been conducted.

Malta had been through the inefficient Italian methods of warfare; she had weathered the initial storm which gained any effect it had mainly from novelty and surprise and had then settled down to an almost normal existence only disturbed by the sporadic Italian bombing raids by day and nuisance "visitors" by night. The initial enthusiasm with which the anti-aircraft gunners had fired their shells into the sky had been curbed as it was realised that in an isolated fortress of this type ammunition replenishment was not just a question of getting on the telephone line to worry an already harassed staff officer. Any replenishments of Malta's stocks meant a major naval operation and the proportionate strengths of the Axis and British fleets in the Mediterranean made any such effort a reckless gamble, having as its only justification a knowledge of the psychology of the Italian sailors.

Italian bombs had fallen on Malta's soil with sufficient inaccuracy to instil in the populace an ardent and enduring hatred of the aggressor. Elaborate plans had been perfected by the Government and by the military authorities for the compulsory evacuation of the crowded areas around the dockyard for it was feared that the population might panic under attack from the air. No such thing occurred, but on the second day after the hate commenced, Valetta and its surrounding towns seemed like a region of the dead. Shops were shut, hardly a soul was to be seen on the street and nothing appeared to be moving except an endless stream of heavily laden carozzin and donkey carts. Piled high with furniture and household goods, this melancholy procession could be seen wending its way in complete good humour and order from the crowded area to the countryside where their relations and friends prepared to receive them. The flight to Gozo became intense and that Island rapidly reached a peak in population, the Maltese believing that it offered a safe refuge from the constant bombing. Quietly and with no fuss, the inhabitants of the affected areas either evacuated themselves or else proceeded to make their homes underground or in shelters hewn by their own hands in the ancient ramparts and bastions of Malta. The Government's elaborate scheme came to nought, but its object was achieved.

But as the weeks went by the Island returned to its normal life, the chief affliction being the lack of mail and news from home. With Britain undergoing its ordeal at the hands of the Luftwaffe the anxieties of all were very great. Cables had been held up sometimes for twelve or fourteen days and for months letters were unknown. Worst blow of all was when a small force of destroyers called in at Malta on a dash through the Mediterranean to England. The accumulated mail from the whole Island was loaded onto one destroyer. It must have proved too much for her because poor HMS "Hostile" struck a mine en route to Gibraltar and foundered taking with her all the mail bags. Luckily, and for this everyone was glad, the loss of life was very light.

The advent of the Huns, however, brought the hard realities of war right to the heart of Malta. Savage bombing, impressive in its intensity and at first in its accuracy, was succeeded by wild and wanton destruction and random aiming of bombs and mines on thickly populated areas, when the Germans realised that accuracy of aim and military damage could only be achieved at great loss to themselves.

Towards the end of the first German onslaught "Kingsway", Valetta's main street, whose name had been changed to this from "Strada Reale" at the insistence of Mabel and her newspaper correspondence column, began to wear a sorry appearance. Large gaps were visible in its structure close to the Cathedral of St. John with all its priceless treasures. But, although severe, the damage when the Germans left was nothing compared to what they were to wreak on their next onslaught.

Convoys passed in and out of the harbours of Malta through the daring and resource of the Royal Navy without any loss up to this time and when the Germans retired from the fray in the early part of May, Malta enjoyed weeks of complete freedom from day attack. By night, however, it was a very different matter, the Italians being adept at maintaining a ceaseless stream of single bombers in order to keep the populace on its toes and the gunners at their duty stations. The searchlights and the night fighters between them achieved many kills but there was no doubt that the population felt happier when they heard the guns roaring up at the approaching invader even though they realized that the number of kills was small in comparison with the amount of noise involved. The same reaction had been noticed when the Germans first turned to night-bombing in their attacks on London. It does the heart good to feel that someone is hitting back and however effective the night fighter tactics or the searchlights may be there is no doubt that the barking of the guns has a strengthening and reassuring effect on the nerves of the population.

The "Times of Malta" run by that dynamic personality, the Hon Mabel Strickland, had continued publication without ceasing, and incidentally was to continue publication without one single break through the desperate months that were to come. The fact that this feat was achieved can only be largely due to Mabel, as she is universally known. Her enthusiasm and intense partisanship of her cause made on many occasions for strained relations between herself and the victims of her assaults and policies, yet no one can deny that her work in keeping up the emotions and patriotism of the Maltese populace was a very large factor in the maintenance of the Island's morale. Later on, in spite of the direct hits which her office received and the destruction of part of the actual press and of all the photographic reproduction apparatus, the "Times of Malta" appeared regularly every morning to bring us news from home and abroad and leading articles couched in Mabel's own inimitable forceful style. Mabel was interested in every facet of life and she is one of the greatest "crusaders" I have ever met. I was lucky enough to know her well and was privileged on several occasions to be a guest in her step-mother's beautiful home in the centre of the Island where the garden was world famous and lovingly tended by Lady Strickland herself who knew every leaf of every plant that grew in its ordered expanse.

The "Times of Malta" was furiously anti-Italian and carried its sentiments to the lengths that it demanded the banning of any form of music by Italian composers. One evening after listening to a beautiful selection of operatic records belonging to Colonel McCombe the DDMS, I wrote this poem which I sent with my compliments to Mabel who gave me tea on the strength of it and told me that she had greatly enjoyed it, but felt it was against her policy to publish.

I was walking about in Headquarters one night
Apprehensively scanning the moon,
When I heard from an office close by on my right
A familiar Italian tune.
Now about such behaviour the press has been sizzling
With letters so full of complaint,
That I wondered who could be this out and out
Quisling
So lacking in any restraint
As to show such contempt for the happenings in
Asia,
(And all that they bring in their train),
That he broadcast the song of the poor little
Geisha
And her naval American swain.
If it's music we need let it be by some master
Who was brought up in Guildford or Fleet,
"Hearts of Oak" is the theme for a national
disaster;
In a crisis—an Eric Coates suite.
For how can we conquer this chap Mussolini,
If we don't make the most of our chances,
And quickly supplant all these airs from Puccini
With Henry the Eighth's famous dances?
The time has gone past for "By God or by guess"
(Leave that to the medical world)
So I rushed to make clear to the DDMS
That the standards of war were unfurled.
Just then he was humming a nice bit of Lieder
(Beating time with a nasty catheter)
Then he calmly broke into "Celeste Aida"
And examined a slide of excreta.
"I'm blacked out" he said, "in the hell of a frowst
And I'm going to play all my Liszt
Then follow it up with selections from Faust
And that song twixt Isolde and Trist.
If we do win this war then it won't be conditional
On music; so listen, do *you* know
I don't think that English composer "Traditional"
Is in the same class as Herr Gounod".

There is a story told against Colonel McCombe which is
worth repeating. He was intensely jealous of the rights,
privileges and prerogatives of the Corps of which he was such
a distinguished member and it is well-known that the RAMC

prefer to be called "Medical Officers" rather than "doctors". One day in Mess somebody happened to remark that the Doctors did not agree to something. Colonel McCombe drew himself up to his full height, which was very impressive, and said "I will not have my officers described as Doctors". He realised his mistake as soon as the remark was out of his mouth by the shout of joy that greeted it.

Now that we have reached lighter things let us examine what had been done in the way of recreation and entertainment for the beleagured garrison.

On the outbreak of war a group of stranded cabaret artistes who were doing the Mediterranean round collected together and devised a touring concert party which was the first to perform, apart from our own MADC concert parties which had had to stop when war actually broke out and we were forced to remain at our war stations. The quality of the show was not very great and the humour was robust to say the least, but they did do an immense amount of good, were sponsored by NAAFI and sent round to the various outposts continuing their tours for many months.

Then the RAF set up a rival concert party known as the "Raffians". These were led by a professional entertainer and his equally talented wife who had been in the Island when hostilities broke out. He joined the RAF immediately and his work in entertainment and production of various theatrical enterprises was done entirely as an addition to his RAF service, while his wife was also employed on radio location duties. This party achieved a very high standard of excellence and was welcomed wherever it went, finally producing on two successive Christmases a really first class pantomime which the whole Island attended.

Finally in the way of theatrical entertainment there came our own efforts of which I have already written.

For outdoor entertainment apart from bathing there was little opportunity. In an excess of enthusiasm on the outbreak of hostilities the Marsa golf course had been ploughed up and converted into allotments. There were no facilities for riding in the Island and the number of playing fields available was grossly inadequate for the number of teams that wished to use them. Shortage of transport made it very difficult to collect teams for any form of sport and the men and officers were largely left to their own devices to seek relaxation. Strait Street, or "The Gut" as it was more familiarly known, flourished with its collection of cheap tinsel attractions, dubious drinks and doubtful reputation, but the soldier could go there and obtain a meal and a drink and take part in dancing for a very small expenditure. At the three establishments reserved for officers one could get the same drinks for the privilege of paying approximately four times the price, and if the truth were to be told, the atmosphere was sordid in the extreme and only bearable if one explored it when one was well primed. However, there was one character universally known as "Auntie", the proprietress of "Auntie's" and reputed to be the sister of a famous English actress. She continued to run her establishment with her curious combination of generosity and high prices. The mention of any senior Naval officers' name to her probably only recalled a vision of a very junior "two striper" who had patronised her bar many years before. She certainly claimed to know them all and everyone was "darling" to her after five minutes' acquaintance.

The heat of Malta in summer is too great to allow of any indoor entertainment and so K Warren and a band of friends embarked upon an outdoor production of James Bridie's play "Tobias and the Angel". They found an ideal spot for it in the gardens surmounting Malta's ramparts and there was deep disappointment when Archbishop Caruana vetoed the production at the very last moment on the grounds that it was a religious subject. Strenuous efforts were vainly made to persuade him to change his mind, but in spite of the fact that it was stressed that the story came from the Apocrypha, he remained adamant and the project had to be abandoned on the very eve of its production. It was really bad luck on K who had worked so hard and who had chosen just the right time of year and day to achieve the delicate lighting that was so essential for the beautiful mise-en-scene.

Writing of Archbishop Caruana, now alas dead, reminds me that as yet nothing has been said of that great stalwart of the Roman Catholic Church. He had been the head of the Church in Malta for many years, having originally been Archbishop of Rhodes. It was his wise guidance and support of the Allied cause that was such a help in smoothing over the difficulties that were encountered in the early days of war, when church buildings and even churches themselves had to be requisitioned for military purposes. I only had the privilege of knowing him when he was old and in failing health, but even then it was an experience to meet him and to listen to his judgements on men and affairs and enjoy his sense of humour which always kept pace with the topics of the moment. His voice when he officiated at any festival was so true and his enunciation so clear that it was difficult to believe that he was not twenty years younger than his actual age. He participated in many religious functions that I attended and he will always remain in my memory as an outstanding example of what a great prelate should be. One felt that he was at one and the same time a priest and yet fully able to appreciate and understand the frailties of more average men. His successor Monsignor Gonzi, who had been Bishop of Gozo, is also widely travelled and capable of speaking many languages to perfection.

The religious enthusiasm of the Maltese people can only be appreciated by those who have experienced it. Wherever they go they set up their little shrines and hold masses and the number of enormous churches in the Island built by the willing hands of the inhabitants of each village is probably the first salient feature that impresses itself on the mind of the new arrival. True to tradition, the Maltese did not forget their God when they descended into the earth to take shelter from the onslaught from the air. I visited several of these deep underground caves. They were surprisingly clean and well ordered and there was not one without its little chapel or shrine specially set aside where the priest came and preached and where the people continued to offer up their prayers during the actual progress of the raids. The populace made special heroes of General Dobbie, the Governor, and of those gallant pilots who first took the air in those out-of-date Gladiators and prayers were always being offered up for their safety.

Generally, the population slept underground and stayed above ground during the day, but at convoy times when raids in force were anticipated whole families could be seen transferring their more portable goods and chattels down to their allotted niches in the shelter. However, during that lazy summer the Italians gave little reason for such permanent cave dwelling and the only large scale offensive that they made at all was the "E" boat attack which has already been described. Life seemed normal again: the Germans had, temporarily at any rate, and at that moment nobody anticipated their return, retired from the fray and the Wops gave nobody any anxiety with their futile methods of attack. It was, therefore, with little inkling of the stern days to come that I said a sad Goodbye to Brigadier Sadler and the 7th AA Brigade and returned to the heat of Valetta and the stuffy offices of War Headquarters.

*   *   *   *   *   *

The arrival of any new Commander almost always involves a re-organisation taking place as a result of the impact of a fresh approach to the problem or situation. The arrival of the new CRA in Malta had proved no exception to this rule and the first problem with which I was greeted on becoming his chief staff officer was the preparation of an operation instruction incorporating his changes in policy. My predecessor had left voluminous notes but unfortunately his writing was even worse than my own and after three quarters of an hour of intense eye-strain I gave up trying to read it and decided to throw myself on the mercy of the CRA and get the policy from him. This was my first experience of writing operation instructions on the higher level and I should have failed miserably if it had not been for his help and guidance. I little thought as I struggled to draft it that I should remain in the job sufficiently long to complete eighty-four others before I finally handed over to my successor. Dame Fortune was undoubtedly on my side at this juncture as two days after I assumed the appointment it was upgraded to the rank of Lieutenant Colonel.

With the great expansion of the artillery in Malta the size of its staff had to be increased and the office accommodation problem became acute. Finally it was decided that the whole of the RA staff should leave War HQ and return to the Castile at the entrance to Valetta. This was one of the Auberges of Malta and had a most exquisite exterior, which still remains almost intact in spite of the fact that almost the entire interior was completely destroyed in the Spring of 1942. Griff Kewley, the staff captain, set to work on the task of fixing up accommodation and offices with great energy and within a fortnight we were magnificently and comfortably installed.

In this short interval the position of AADC had fallen vacant as it seemed to be no longer required with two Brigadiers in the Island specially deputed to study the AA problems. The third Artillery Brigade, by the way, which controlled the Coast Artillery, was commanded at that time by Brigadier G. C. Gatt who was the first member of the Royal Malta Artillery to reach that exalted rank. The Gatt family and the Royal Malta Artillery are intimately inter-related as there were many sons of the Brigadier almost all of whom had entered the ranks of that old established Regiment. Suddenly news was received from the War Office that a Colonel Woolley was on his way out to us as AADC. This created a slight problem as he was a full Colonel and therefore senior to me on the staff. The difficulty was resolved by the CRA who decided that Col Woolley would be his advisor on AA and searchlight matters while I should remain his senior staff officer. This arrangement worked admirably the entire time that Col Woolley was there, and his help, advice and careful consideration of policy linked with the unostentatious way in which he set out to help was of the greatest assistance to us all and I for one was always deeply grateful to him.

In October a submarine arrived in the harbour, bringing with it a new officer who had come from England to join his old master the CRA. George Wishart and I have often laughed since at the disreputable spectacle he presented on his arrival. The paraffin fumes from the submarine's innards had affected his eyes so that they were red-rimmed and weeping copiously. Neither is a submarine the cleanest place in which to travel, and so it was with some trepidation that I took this sorry object to lunch at the Union Club. I was to learn in the eighteen months that followed what a tower of strength and loyalty George was to prove, and his contribution to the well-being of the gunners and the revitalising of the Garrison after the months of intense strain, was something of which he will always have every reason to be proud.

The CRA fully appreciated the vital importance of morale and one of the first steps he took to give everyone a pride in the formation to which they belonged was to have shoulder flashes designed for HQ RA and the three Brigades. They were all of the same pattern involving a Maltese Cross in various colours on a black background. In the case of HQ RA and the field artillery regiments the colours were the gunner colours of red and blue, for the two AA Brigades the colours of gunpowder (blue and yellow) and for the Coast Artillery Brigade, which was largely Maltese, the cross was composed of a combination of Malta's own colours, red and white. These shoulder flashes were ordered from home and when they arrived were worn with pride. On their return to England many members of the RA who have been in Malta have still clung to these shoulder flashes in spite of having left the Island.

One of the establishments in Malta which had constantly kept open and catered for the service man's needs was the British Institute. Under its auspices there was organised a series of orchestral concerts with two conductors, Maestro Nani who was Malta's premier civil conductor and Maestro Bellizzi who was conductor of the Vice Admiral's band. On Friday afternoons the concert hall in the British Institute would be packed to overflowing and magnificent performances were rendered by this full-scale symphony orchestra. We became regular attendants at these concerts and helped to swell the orchestra by the loan of many members of the band of the Royal Artillery, Malta, which also helped to raise our self-esteem as a regiment.

A more official form of raising morale was the mounting of a military guard on the entrance to the Castile. Each Artillery Regiment in turn produced this guard which had to

The ceremony of the mounting of the RA Guard at the Castille, Valetta.

be faultlessly turned out and drilled. The mounting ceremony took place on Tuesday of each week at five o'clock on the Castile square. The Royal Artillery Malta band attended and each regiment brought with it one piece of its equipment (for instance a HAA Regiment would bring a 3.7" gun or a LAA Regiment a Bofor and tractor) and these guns were left on the square for the population to inspect after the ceremony was over. Even the Coast Artillery were able to bring a gun with them as a mobile reserve was formed of some old Naval guns in case a fort should be bombed out of action. The care and trouble which all the regiments took to ensure that their gun was the best painted and the best polished on parade resulted in a general heightening of the standard of maintenance throughout each unit. Obviously no Section or Battery Commander would allow his guns to be in worse condition than any other unit within his formation.

The standard of paintwork and polish was magnificent on all types of guns but perhaps the most interesting exhibits on parade to the population were the searchlights. They undoubtedly always created great enthusiasm when they appeared as a large proportion of them, as well of course, as of the AA and Coast Artillery, were manned by Maltese personnel.

After the ceremony was over the band would play a selection of light music for half an hour and soon a large crowd would collect every Tuesday to see the display. The idea caught on and there were similar ceremonies in other parts of the Island by other units, but the RA guard mounting parade remained a feature of life in Malta until the destruction of the Castile in April 1942. It was resumed early in the same summer and for all I know may be continuing still. One anecdote arises from this. In December it was proposed to include the "1812 Overture" in honour of the Russian successes in stemming the advance on Moscow. Unfortunately the day when this was due to be played, followed the day on which the Japs bombed Pearl Harbour and someone enquired whether we were going to include also a selection from "Madame Butterfly".

Just about this time I received a shoal of congratulatory telegrams from home. I was quite unaware of any reason for this until I was told that Lt-Col Victor Cazalet whom I had met on his first visit with General Sikorski to Malta, had broadcast an account of his stay and in it he mentioned "a senior staff officer aged thirty-one who helped to keep up the morale of the Island by producing plays and concerts in his spare time despite the constant raids and bombs". Someone else must have told him about them as we never mentioned them in our conversations but I was very glad of the "puff" for the sake of the MADC as without the backing of that Club no amount of enthusiasm would have been of any avail.

Every year in Malta there is a big Poppy Day Ball at the British Institute and allied with that are various dances and auctions for the troops of which all the proceeds are given to Earl Haig's Fund. Nick Harrison and myself were deputed to be the auctioneers at the British Institute two years running and the first year one of our lines of business was a small pig. To our horror in the middle of the auction this pig escaped and ran amok in the audience but was finally safely retrieved and handed to its purchaser.

Mention of this charitable function reminds me that early on in the battle a subscription fund had been opened by the "Times of Malta" to buy fighters to help to take part in the Battle of Britain. Malta is not a rich little Island and was a long way from the scene of the Battle of Britain and so it was very creditable that in a short space of time a total of £12,090 was collected which served to purchase two Spitfires christened "Malta" and "Ghaudex" (the ancient name for Gozo) respectively.

A relief fund for the bombed out inhabitants of Malta was also opened and resulted in a total of £23,873 being collected when the first appeal was closed. Later on General Dobbie broadcast a world wide appeal for help for the distressed people of Malta in the face of the intense air attacks and this second appeal brought in over £140,000 making a total of £164,000. A third fund which was liberally subscribed to in Malta was opened as a result of the heavy losses in the convoys bringing supplies to the Island in August 1942. This was only open for a short time, but resulted in a total of £7,500 being subscribed to help the dependents of those who had sacrificed their lives in their efforts to ensure Malta's safety.

There were remarkably few facilities for the entertainment of officers in Malta and so a club was opened next door to the garrison library, under the auspices of HQ Command. The club was called "Maxims" and in October it had a stupendous opening night. The place was filled to overflowing with representatives of all the services and it settled down from the start to be a success. One could obtain almost any kind of drink there at that time and snack meals were served in the restaurant while dancing went on upstairs. It certainly filled a very necessary want and its loss was greatly felt when it was severely damaged by bomb blast and the shortages of any form of alcohol or food caused it to close early in the following year.

Malta was always short of something and one of our chief worries in the gunners was lack of manpower within the Island. Our AA Batteries were on a very low establishment and were being manned for very long hours. Our Coast Artillery was cut down to the bone and it was not possible to find sufficient men in each fort to keep the guns firing at the same time as providing local protection in the event of invasion. It was decided, therefore, to try and recruit some Maltese personnel to act as local defence platoons for each fort and an offer was made to the CRA by an Infantry Brigadier of certain of his personnel whom he described as excellent soldiers but not quite fit for mobile warfare. Brigadier Beckett decided to look this gift horse in the mouth and he went out to see the personnel who had been collected in one assembly centre. Apparently they were all of very low medical category and quite unsuitable, through no fault of their own, for any form of soldiering. The CRA returned and announced that "Not even by the Pool of Siloam had he seen such misery". He considered that "only one officer was fitted to command them and that was Captain Lazarus", and he recommended that "billets be found for them in Abraham's Bosom". This summing up of the situation caused consternation when it was delivered at the GOC's weekly conference, but it had its effect as very shortly a more suitable class of soldier was recruited and trained for this purpose.

Towards the end of November a daylight raid occurred. This was the first daylight raid since May and was, I think, the first of that kind which the CRA had seen in Malta. The 'planes flew right over Valetta in close formation, dropped their bombs in the dockyard area and departed again. Through lack of recent practice in visual shooting the firing of the AA Artillery was wild and little damage was caused to the raiders. We had been outside watching the raid and the effect of the firing. Suddenly the CRA appeared saying: "Why haven't we shot them down?" Up till then I think the general feeling was that it was a good show if a 'plane was brought down, but here was a commander who took the opposite view and expected them to he brought down, thinking it was a bad show if they weren't. We looked at each other wondering whether he would have liked them brought down actually in the Castile Square and lined up ready for inspection but there was no doubt that he was dead right in his view. Everyone "buckled to" determined not to allow many more opportunities for such criticism.

The latter part of November saw the beginning of the crescendo in the scale of air attack which was to reach its mighty climax in April 1942, and this daylight raid was the first manifestation of the Axis determination to reduce Malta by over-whelming bombing attacks. Night raiding had, of course, continued throughout the summer and various tactics had been tried to compete it. For some time the night defence of the Island was left to a combination of searchlights and fighters, but Malta was too small to allow of very many opportunities of holding the raider for long enough to allow the fighter to get onto its tail, and in every case the bomber was only shot down after it had dropped its bombs.

The CRA, therefore, pressed vigorously for a combination of night fighter and AA defences to be employed and gradually this came to be adopted but the RAF insisted on the right to veto AA fire if any of their 'planes would be endangered by it. Malta during that summer had become a large scale RAF offensive base and Wellingtons operated nightly from its various aerodromes. Unfortunately one night a lone raider came over the harbour at the same time as a RAF 'plane was up on test. AA fire was withheld with disastrous results as for the first time, by an unlucky chance, the bomber scored a direct hit and HM Destroyer Maori was sunk, luckily without great loss of life.

This brought the Navy in on our side in the struggle to allow greater AA defence at night, and so, after close liaison and negotiation with the RAF, a system of layers of fighter and AA defence was evolved which gave the best possible protection to the Island with the minimum hindrance either to the RAF offensive operations or to the scope of AA Artillery. In broad principles this arrangement stood the test of time and although many changes had to be made in it to suit various operating conditions, it came to be accepted by both the RAF and the AA gunners and was undoubtedly a very important factor in the improvement of Malta's defences.

The close of the year had brought to Malta a vivid personality in the form of Major-General D. M. W. Beak, VC, DSO, MC, who arrived to take over the command of the Garrison from Major-General Scobell. General Beak certainly minced no words and wasted no time in ordering a drastic re-organisation of the infantry defences against attack from the sea and land. The old idea, largely forced on his predecessor through lack of adequate reserves, of static defence with concrete pill-boxes along the coast and rigidly defined zones of responsibility gave way, almost overnight, to a more mobile conception of defence against an enemy landing. A thin screen was maintained along the beaches and in places where a strong defence could be offered by automatic weapon fire, while the bulk of the troops were held in rear, ready to strike in force at the main landing wherever it came. Even in the midst of all these responsibilities, General Beak found time to pay visits to the Royal Artillery and Royal Malta Artillery Units manning the guns to compliment them on their work and turn-out, and to be a welcome guest at our Mess, where we entertained him with good food, plenty of drink, and a succession of bawdy songs around the piano.

Another function that he attended was the St. Andrew's night dinner. This was organised, with the enthusiastic approval of the CRA (who dug out some Scots ancestry especially for the occasion), by the Scottish officers of a LAA Regiment in the Island. It was held at the Sliema Club. Even haggis was produced, and the evening was enlivened by the performance of Major Fleetwood on his bagpipes. I had known the Fleetwoods for some number of years, having met them first in 1926 in Switzerland. They happened to be in Malta visiting their son and daughter-in-law when war broke out. Without a moment's hesitation Major Fleetwood, who was no longer young, volunteered and was accepted for the Royal Artillery, and almost immediately took up an operational post on an AA position. He remained there for nearly a year, and finally was transferred to Ricasoli Depot, to become the Commanding Officer of the Recruiting and Training Centre there where he continued to do excellent service. But what also made that St. Andrew's night memorable for us was that the other guest of honour was Commander David Wanklin, VC, the ace submarine commander. "Wanks", who had quietly dined in our mess about a month before without saying a word about his award of the VC of that very day, was a legend to everyone in Malta. His exploits are, of course, renowned throughout the world, and were only rivalled by his complete modesty and the devotion which he inspired in all with whom he served. The news of his death a few months later affected the whole Island. It seemed impossible to believe that one so gallant and of such splendid character had had to pay the supreme sacrifice.

As may well be realised, in an Island which has practically no natural resources and is beleagured by the enemy, it was difficult to arrange for any Christmas festivities for the children who abound there. Suzanne Parlby, a daughter of Admiral Layton, one day chanced to suggest that some means should be devised of making toys for the kids. Now the hours of leisure of the soldier in that garrison were very difficult to fill. Transport was out of the question owing to the petrol rationing, and the vast majority found themselves stuck out in the middle of the country with only five or six companions, living in what are known as Elephant Shelters. The CRA seized upon this remark and said " The Gunners will make the toys." The result was that the day before Christmas a most magnificent collection of toys, over two thousand, was on view, all made by the soldiers out of their own local resources.

They ranged from accurate scale models of MTBs down to the inevitable Spitfires and motor cars, and included two magnificent forts, complete with model soldiers made from bully beef tins, and one working model of the interior of a theatre. One Wellington Bomber was so large and so beautiful that it was presented to the AOC as a gesture of goodwill from the gunners. The ingenuity that the soldiers had displayed was something to marvel at, and there were very few of the toys that Hamleys would not have been proud to sell in the days of extravagance before the war.

In addition to the arrival of the new General one or two other changes had taken place. Brigadier Gatt having reached the age limit retired and was made the first Maltese Colonel Commandant, RA and my old CO Colonel White (after having a short spell as Major) succeeded him as Commander Fixed Defences, entering into that new appointment with all his customary enthusiasm. He chose as his Brigade Major an officer from the same Regiment, known universally as "Fish", who had been a friend of mine since shortly after my arrival in Malta. Both "Fish" and C. J. White were adepts at gadgets, and maintained the closest liaison with their naval confreres. So much so that they went "on watch" and slept in "cabins" and practically called it "going ashore" whenever they went to have lunch out of the office. The Brigadier was speedily christened "Admiral White" and "the bridge" in his control room soon contained a most formidable array of switches and lights and other devices.

And so, with this background of welfare, personalities, tactics and politics, we embarked on those eventful months of January to May 1942, when the fate of Malta, and perhaps, some aver, of the whole Mediterranean theatre, trembled in the balance as the little Island shook to the holocaust of bombs launched against it.

CHAPTER VII

Crescendo

THE battle for Malta really began in mid December. A single JU 88 was seen early in the month on reconnaissance over the Island. This was the first German 'plane that had come over by day since the end of the battles of the previous Spring. It put everybody on their mettle. The days of fooling about with the Italians had gone. The advent of the Germans meant the stern realities of war, with no quarter asked, and no quarter given. Shortly after this, Nick Harrison and I were talking in the Castile Square when suddenly we heard a familiar whine. I queried Nick saying: "Surely that is an ME?" We both turned round in time to see a single ME 109 with a yellow nose, flying down the length of the harbour with its guns blazing, and at enormous speed. Nick, who was expert at these things, said at once that he thought it was a ME 109F, which was the very latest German fighter. If this were true, it boded ill for the RAF in Malta, as not only was Malta's airfields space largely given up to bombers, but the fighters we had would be outclassed by this type of Messerschmitt.

We had felt for some time that the Axis could not indefinitely ignore the inroads made on their shipping by the cruisers that had come to be based on Malta. "Aurora" under Captain Agnew, "Penelope" under Captain Nicholl, and "Neptune" under Captain O'Connor had been carrying out the most successful raids on their lines of communication. "Aurora" and Captain Agnew still live to tell the story, but "Neptune", with almost all her gallant crew, was mined and sunk off the coast of Africa, while "Penelope" earned undying fame for the weight of attack she endured in Malta, and her dash through "bomb alley" to the comparative freedom of Gibraltar and beyond. Alas, this gallant ship, after being repaired was fated to be lost in the allied landings on the coast of Italy.

About the 16th December the Germans opened the ball with a sharp raid on the dockyard area. But it was not until Christmas Eve that one was able to perceive the pattern behind the daily raids that had occurred, or to sense the determination with which the plan was going to be carried out. Christmas Day was observed as a holiday by all, but on Boxing Day the Huns again bombed in earnest. Their tactics were excellent from their point of view. They had two major objects to achieve. Firstly, to knock out the rather meagre fighter defences of the Island, and secondly to prevent the cruisers from continuing their marauding sorties. And so, throughout the last of December, and the month of January, they proceeded to send over frequent raids each day. There were never very many bombers in each of these assaults, perhaps five or seven, but the fighter escort was overwhelming, and the number of the raids was very great. By this means they hoped to keep the RAF fighters constantly in the air, so that eventually, those they did not shoot down through sheer force of numbers would be worn out through lack of opportunity for the necessary maintenance. Right gallantly did our pilots pit themselves against the enemy in this uneven struggle, but their armament was woefully outclassed. There were no cannon fighters in Malta in those days, but time after time we would see a gallant pilot burst his way through the screen of Messerschmitts, get close in to one of the JU 88s, and seemingly pour all hell into him. Yet the armour of these 'planes seemed to be able to resist the attacks, and in a great number of cases a German 'plane would return safely to its base after these encounters when it would have been a sure kill for a fighter equipped with cannon. By mingling these constant raids on aerodromes with attacks on the harbour, the Germans also forced the cruisers to expend considerable quantities of AA ammunition and kept the ships in a state of perpetual alert. They continued these tactics throughout January, when the weather, as so often during this war, was very favourable to them. It was a peculiarly cloudy month and those bombers were able to make repeated trips to Malta, take every advantage of cloud cover and remain comparatively unscathed. During the whole month of January, in spite of the number of raids, only eleven 'planes were destroyed for certain over Malta, six by fighters and five by AA.

In February it was obvious that the German plan was yielding dividends. The number of fighters put up against them began to dwindle, and shortly the maintenance situation became so serious that our fighters would remain grounded for some of the raids so that they could take the air in some force for the remainder. Bearing this in mind, the Germans stepped up their scale of bombing. Not only did they increase the number of raids each day, but they also increased the number of bombers in each visitation. In order not to be left entirely out of the picture, the Italians carried on with their nuisance raids by night. Nor was this night raiding just a token effort, as is revealed by the fact that during one night sixty-four enemy planes crossed the coast.

This continual attack placed an immense strain on the personnel of the AA Artillery. At one period, out of seventy-two hours the guns were manned for sixty-six. Human endurance cannot go on for ever, and eventually a system of reliefs had to be devised, so that the men could get adequate sleep and rest. The number of men available on each gun position was only just sufficient to man the guns, and so it was a case of having to put one gun out of action at a time. Should a very large scale raid be plotted as coming in during that time, provision was made for the men to be recalled from their rest, but every effort was made to avoid this course. On the whole this system of reliefs did provide the necessary rest for the sorely tried gun detachments. It was just about this time that a mail came in from home containing, amongst other things, the War Establishment for a Heavy AA Battery in the UK. As opposed to our meagre one hundred and eighty men in all, the home establishment allowed one hundred and eighty-two men and one hundred and eighty women. Comment was immediate—"What do the other two do?"

To give some idea of the continuity of the attack, it may be of interest to mention that on one day in February we had seventeen raids in twenty-four hours. From the 3rd March to the 10th March three-quarters of the entire time was taken up with raids, and actually, during the whole of March the total numbers of hours spent under raids added up to exactly fifteen days, i.e. half the month. The longest raid we ever had was one which lasted for thirteen and a quarter hours, and the worst day was on the 8th/9th March, when out of twenty-four hours twenty-one and a half were devoted by the Luftwaffe to destroying Malta.

What we badly needed, of course, were Spitfires. These 'planes that had struck terror into the hearts of the German pilots in the Battle of Britain would, with their cannon, have proved an able match for the Messerschmitts. As it was, despite all the gallantry in the world, our fighters were outclassed and outnumbered and it was with our hearts in our mouths that we watched them, or listened to them, droning upwards into the sky against such terrible odds. However, even though fighters might come to Malta, the Island could not exist indefinitely without replenishing its stocks of ammunition and of foodstuffs. In March, therefore, a convoy was sailed from Alexandria. Two days before its arrival some fighter reinforcements were flown off an aircraft carrier in the Western Mediterranean to give the protection so vital for the oncoming ships. The 'planes arrived on the morning and afternoon of 20th March, and the German reaction was almost instantaneous. At dusk, after fifteen previous alerts that day the air alarm sounded once more, and there then ensued one of the most awe inspiring sights we had ever seen. This was no ordinary bombing raid. Wave after wave of JU 88s came out of the north with almost clockwork precision, to swoop low over Ta Kali aerodrome where the Spitfires were being serviced. If the safety of these 'planes had not been of such importance to the well-being of the convoy one would have watched with admiration the tactics and the timing of this attack. The light was just dark enough to hide the approach of the bombers until they roared down onto their targets, and yet when the searchlights attempted to pick them up it was not sufficiently dark for them to be of use. If anything, their searching beams only added to the difficulties of the spotters. It was a terrific attack, even though it cost the Germans some fourteen 'planes. It very nearly succeeded in wiping out the fighter reinforcements which had been caught on the ground, and made the task of protecting the convoy a hazardous one indeed.

The men on the Light AA guns around the aerodrome and in infantry defences had, of course, to bear the brunt of this attack, but casualties proved to be unbelievably light after that heavy mass raid. Almost directly after the "all clear" we got yet another alert and Nick came to me saying: "It is five hundred plus." I looked at him and said: "What does that mean?" He replied: "Well, I think this is it, or else it is a peculiar cloud reaction on the machine". Mercifully, it turned out to be the latter, but it could hardly have come at a more inauspicious moment. The next morning the Huns took up the tune once more and at about breakfast time he produced another raid of the same dimensions, this time diving out of the sun onto that same little airfield of Ta Kali. His losses continued, but even so the weight of attack was a terrific strain on the courage of the men on the aerodrome defences who had to face up to it. So, early in the afternoon "Otto" Smaile and I drove out to do a tour of the LAA positions and to see in what way we could be of help to them.

Everyone is afraid of death, or at any rate of the anticipation of death. It is so very final and the uncertainty of what lies beyond is not soothing to the mind. In war time death generally comes suddenly, and one has no time for heroic thoughts or weakness at the knees, but that afternoon at Ta Kali I believed that death would inevitably claim us in a minute at most. As we left one position we were told that an attack was building up but we never dreamt that anything would eventuate before we could get to the next gun and take our position in the gunpit. However, as we passed the cemetery on the edge of the landing ground the heavy guns opened up in earnest. We looked up and to our horror the sky seemed black with bombers winging their way steadily towards us. At any moment they would dive and unload their cargoes of death. There is something very inexorable about the approach of bombers. One sees them in the distance as little specks and gradually they loom larger and larger. There is nothing one can do. They have got to be allowed to approach until they come within range and it is during these tense moments before one can spring into action that the strain tells most. The initiative lies with the enemy. It is he who calls the tune and the detachments on the smaller calibre weapons can only wait until the enemy comes so very close, and by then he has probably launched his missiles against them. Once one can start hitting back all feeling of fear goes, but if one has no active means of defence or the wait is long before they dive, the strain allows the imagination to give vent to too vivid pictures. On this occasion neither of us had any weapon and the only protection near us was a gutter some six inches deep at the side of the road bounding the airfield itself. We did not linger to see them dive, but in company with a RAF Corporal we wedged ourselves into this gutter as low as we could.

It seemed an eternity as we waited for the first whistle. Otto was quite quiet, but the RAF Corporal was praying sufficiently hard to suffice for the three of us. I gave a short prayer that death might be instantaneous and fell to regretting many of the aims and ambitions I knew I would never fulfil. Then it came, the first whistle of a bomb falling on the aerodrome, on the edge of which we were lying, as flat as nature would allow us. From that moment on whine was succeeded by whine, each growing louder until it did not seem possible that the next one could miss us. Rocket bombs, heavy calibre bombs, anti-personnel bombs seemed to be exploding all round us. Then there was a lull. The first wave was over. "This is a very undignified position isn't it" I said. "Without any of the usual advantages" answered Otto and giggling we buried our heads again as a second avalanche began. This time we were straddled both crosswise and lengthwise, and debris fell all over us. I was shaken, and felt that the tension must be relieved. "I never made such a close study of ants before" I shouted in a temporary lull. "I have got two up my nose" he yelled back. As if infuriated at these trivialities the Huns loosed off a rocket bomb which roared to earth too close to be comfortable. Dust again became our staple diet.

I remember seeing the cemetery hit and thinking what little trouble we would cause. Here we were, just by it, and that bomb must surely have dug a grave for us. In one pause we caught a glimpse of two parachutists from a blazing bomber drifting to earth through the barrage of shot and shell. There were more bombers to come, and it struck me as a grim jest that they would probably be killed in the next attack from their own 'planes. At last the noise died down. The dust pall lifted and we rose to our feet. It had not been pleasant, but it was something to look back upon. If ever again I am fated to undergo a similar experience I trust I shall have the benefit of Otto's calm humour, and the comfort of our companion's prayers. There will then be little to worry about in this world or the next!

In the twenty-four hours in which these attacks took place it is interesting to note that the Luftwaffe dropped two hundred and ninety tons of bombs onto one small little aerodrome. During the same week we read of how the air offensive had been maintained against Germany. It was only later that we discovered that our bombers had dropped in the course of that week two hundred and ninety tons on the whole of Germany. Those days are past now, and a raid of such dimensions is only chicken feed, but it did not seem so to us at the time.

Meanwhile, the convoy, battered from the air and threatened by surface ships and submarines, was steadily heading for Malta, protected and guarded by the audacious tactics of Admiral Vian. Eventually, it came into sight on the 23rd March, and three ships safely made fast in the Grand Harbour. But the fourth ship was the one we were all anxious about. HMS Breconshire, which had become the idol of Malta, was hit off Zonkor Point in the last couple of miles of her journey. It was a small bomb from a fighter bomber, but it had struck her in the engine room, destroying both her engines and the power for pumping out the inrushing sea. Perhaps I may be forgiven if I tell the story of HMS Breconshire as I wrote it for the "Times of Malta" on the 1st April, 1942 and for which both Admiral Leatham (the VAM) and Captain Hutchinson, the Captain of the ship, expressed their gratitude. I was not to know then that she would have kept her trust so faithfully as, even after she was sunk, a considerable quantity of her cargo and all the salvageable oil that she carried was safely landed on the Island.

HMS BRECONSHIRE—A TRIBUTE

(This article was published in the "Times of Malta" on 1st April, 1942)

BIRTH

After months of speculation and premature publicity the great day had arrived, and what had been a pious hope would at last begin to take shape. "The pleasure of your company is requested at the laying down of the keel, etc., etc". Thus ran the invitation, and right gladly did we wend our way to the Taikoo Dock. For this ship was to be a challenge—a challenge to Japan. It was to be the first of several fast passenger-carrying cargo ships to compete with the Japanese mercantile marine. England was tardily waking up to the reality of the menace to her maritime trade. And it was to be the first ship of over 10,000 tons ever to be built in Hong Kong.

So, in the company of Tai-pans and coolies, Ruth Draper-like matrons and Cantonese maidens, rickshaws and taxis, we found ourselves at the ceremony. And as we gazed at the mass of scaffolding and cranes that lay higgledy piggledy in front of our eyes, our thoughts winged into the future. From the apparent chaos in front of us, order was being achieved. Instead of oily cranes and sweating coolies we saw a stately ship emerging from the dock to sail the seven seas and fly the red ensign proudly in foreign ports. What stories would that ship be able to tell when finally her turn came to be sold to the ship-breakers? Tales of lovers holding hands on the boat deck beneath a tropical moon? Tales of heartbreak, of separation, and, perhaps, of the joy of reunion? Stirring epics of rescue or of battles with the elements? Or would they just be tales of commercial enterprise, of employment given to thousands, and, at the end, the recapture for Britain of the riches of the trade routes, even though it was only through iron ore, Tyne coal and cheap tin trays? Whatever they would be, she was a pioneer, the first of her kind, and the first to be built in Britain's farthest outpost, the nearest to Japan. This alone constituted her first challenge.

The keel was laid, hospitality and refreshment drove away speculation as to the future, and again the present had us in its grip. But the day would not be far distant when she would take the water and so "Good luck to her, and all who sail in her".

Salute to a brave enterprise.

MATURITY

Some three years later an armed merchant ship slipped into the Grand Harbour of Valetta, to the accompaniment of gaily waving handkerchiefs and clapping crowds on the famous Baraccas of Malta. "Mare Nostrum" had proved a vain boast for the Italian Navy and the Regia Aeronautica. The Luftwaffe had been forced to bolster up their bubble of bombastic pride. The Germans proved determined pilots, and the Mediterranean grew perilous for our shipping. But again and again the bubble had been pricked by this gallant ship and equally gallant captain and crew. She was flying the White Ensign now, not the red that we had seen in imagination. She was still a challenge to a foreign nation, not in peaceful rivalry but in all the dangers and hazards of war. She was pitting herself not against Japan but against Germany and Italy, and by her efforts was not only maintaining the essential commodities for beleaguered Malta, but also the morale of all who knew her. The Island base of Malta took to her bosom the ship whose birthplace was another Island base far away off the coast of China, so soon to become war-scarred in her turn. No-one ever doubted her. When she left us to run the gauntlet of the Mediterranean, no-one questioned whether she would get through. It was unthinkable that she should not arrive at her destination, or that very soon we should not see her again. And every time she justified that faith.

Salute to a brave ship.

DEATH

She was lying in Marsaxlokk Bay. Loaded down with stores for Malta, she had battled her way doggedly against the enemy and the elements to within three miles of her allotted berth when she was struck. Now she lay helpless within sight of home, her engine room flooded, but her cargo intact. The Island defences rushed to her aid and protected her throughout a day and a night from the dealers of death in the skies. But they could not aid her against the forces of nature. The sea was too rough to allow her to be towed to safety. Was she going to fail to make port then, after all? Weighed down by cargo and by sea water, with no power to work the pumps, it seemed that she must stagger and fall, as Dorando staggered and fell in the last few yards of his Marathon. But nature relented sufficiently to allow a tow rope to be fastened. In tow she entered Marsaxlokk Bay and tied up to a buoy. She had made port. Even then she was given no respite and shown no mercy till, helpless at her moorings she was hit again by a single heavy calibre bomb from a Stuka after many savage attacks had been warded off her by fighters and gunners alike. The crew fought valiantly for hours to save her, but at last the order came—"Abandon Ship". Even so, the next dawn found her still afloat. Malta was asked, "Could you sink her by shooting?" Can one shoot one's own dog, even if it is in kindness? But the order had to be given and the guns were got ready. Perhaps she heard them, because she disdained their aid. As we reached the top of the hill overlooking her resting-place, we saw her reel over like a tired spaniel in front of a fire, and settle down on her side. She was tired, broken and weary, but she had kept faith.

Salute to a brave death.

CHAPTER VIII

Act II

THESE attacks just prior to the convoy heralded a new era in the aerial warfare against Malta. From now on the continuous raiding by small forces of bombers was to give place to massed raids at almost regular hours each day. The arrival of any convoy would make the Grand Harbour and the ships unloading there a priority target for the enemy, but their anxiety to accomplish the downfall of this particular convoy must have been increased by a series of somewhat unfortunate broadcasts and announcements in England. It was proclaimed that an important convoy had been escorted to Malta containing much ammunition and equipment for the Island. It may have been just coincidence that from that moment these massed raids were concentrated on the harbour. But when a few days later it was announced that the gas works were still operating and the enemy proceeded to destroy them immediately and followed up with attacks on the cinemas and the power station which had also been mentioned as still functioning, people began to wonder. Of course there may not have been any connection between the results the enemy achieved and the pronouncements from England, but those of us on the spot began to pray that nobody else would get up and announce that anything else was undamaged or our days would surely be numbered.

These successes of the enemy were aided by another unfortunate chain of circumstances. "The Breconshire", as already related, had been put out of action only some two or three miles from the entrance to the harbour. Just at this time the CRA was recuperating from an illness and staying at San Anton, the Governor's Palace. It was obviously important from our AA point of view that all the ships should be concentrated under the densest AA umbrella that could be provided. So, as soon as I heard of the mishap to the "Breconshire" I rushed down to see Admiral Leatham, who was conferring with his staff, and stressed to him the urgency of trying to bring the "Breconshire" into either the Grand Harbour, from where she could be given the highest degree of protection, or if the entrance to that was too difficult on account of the rough seas, to berth her in Marsamuscetto Harbour where nearly as good an umbrella could be provided. The Admiral and his staff received me with the utmost courtesy and obviously appreciated the necessity of trying to make the best use of the AA protection. Immediately after my interview with them I dashed out to San Anton to see the CRA who added his weight to the argument that I had put forward. But unfortunately, either the seas were too rough or the difficulties of the minefields were too great, and the decision had to be taken to tow her round to calmer water in the SE corner of the Island. From our point of view, this proved a calamity. The Germans immediately appreciated that the efficacy of the AA would be halved if they put in simultaneous attacks on the ships in harbour and on that valuable lone ship in Marza Scirocco Bay. They carried out this plan with the utmost efficiency, but the fighters and the AA held them off for two days until at last, the inevitable happened and hits were scored on all the ships. The weight of attack proved too great and every ship of that precious convoy was sunk.

But that was not the end of the story. The Infantry Battalions, the chief among them the 1st Battalion of the Cheshire Regiment, leaped into the breach. With a total disregard for their safety they proceeded to go on board these half-sunken ships and unload them, even in the midst of the most intensive attacks and oblivious of the danger from fire and exploding ammunition in the holds, thereby salvaging a large quantity of their invaluable cargo. Thus began a close and intimate association of the Cheshire Regiment with the Dockyard and Grand Harbour which was to last for many months and was commemorated by the unveiling of a placque in the dock-yard ramparts in early 1943. This ceremony was one of the most pleasant that can be imagined as it came as a spontaneous gesture of admiration from the personnel of the dockyard to this gallant battalion which had done so much both in defence of that area and in hard manual labour to improve the efficiency of its working under the most adverse circumstances.

Meanwhile HMS Penelope, the last of the cruisers, was lying damaged in French Creek. Attack after attack was made on her, but adding her welcome quota to the land artillery protection she valiantly resisted them all. As is well known, she sustained so much damage that she became christened "The pepper-pot ship". Finally, one day, it was considered that she was sufficiently seaworthy to make a dash for safety through the Mediterranean. There was breathless anticipation as the hour for her departure drew nigh. Her crew were flogged to the wide with the strain of preparing the ship, manning the armament, and stocking up for the journey. A few hours before she was due to sail yet more heavy attacks were put in against her and the reserves of AA ammunition became too low to last her on her perilous journey to the west. Immediately, and without hesitation, the Cheshires and Maltese dockyard employees proceeded to procure the ammunition and to bring it to the ship side. With this magnificent co-operation she was able to cast off only a short time after schedule and slip away to safety in the dark. The next morning the inevitable raid came in and the operators listening in to the German radio between the bombers had the enormous satisfaction of hearing them say "I can't see the cruiser. The cruiser has gone".

These mass attacks used to come regularly, just about breakfast time, then about lunch time, and finally between five and six in the evening, with very often a mid-afternoon one thrown in as well. Every one of the attacks would contain some seventy-five to eighty bombers, heavily escorted by fighters. Before they came in the fighters would come over the Island, trying to tempt our meagre fighter force into the air, and long after the bombers had departed several relays of fighters remained behind to try and get our pilots as they returned to land. With the best will in the world, no population could remain underground permanently and so a system of signalling was devised. The alert would be sounded when the first 'planes were some thirty miles from the Island. As soon as it became obvious that it was to be a bombing raid a red flag was hoisted between the top of the Castile and Palace towers. Once the bombers had gone the red flag came down and the majority of the populace would come up from the shelters and proceed to get on with cooking the dinner or doing the household chores.

The losses of the enemy began to creep up in March. Their bold tactics could not be carried out without taking extra risks and both fighters and AA took full advantage of their chances. Sixty-two 'planes in all, thirty-four by the RAF and twenty-eight by the AA were destroyed during the month of March, and many others probably never struggled home. The enemy strategy was obviously to soften up the Island before the invasion took place. At first, as already related, the enemy made the aerodromes his main objective, but once the danger from fighter attack had decreased he proceeded deliberately to attack the fringes of the aerodromes where he hoped to destroy the Light AA and Infantry LMG positions. The dockyard, of course, came in for its full share of the weight of bombs and rapidly became a shambles. He followed these tactics up by concentrated attacks on the Heavy AA and Coast Artillery positions and then finally he proceeded to bomb all the main roads and communication centres. Even so, he was beginning to be infuriated by his losses and commenced to vent his rage deliberately on the built-up areas and prominent buildings.

I remember well the first deliberate attack on Valetta. We were standing on the roof of one of the ancient fortifications watching the bombers come in. We suddenly noticed that they were pursuing a different course from any previous line taken by them. They were approaching directly up the line of the peninsula on which Valetta stands. I said to Nick and the others: "I don't like the look of this. We had better take cover." Nick hesitated for a minute and so I gave him the only direct order in the whole of our time together. He came along with us and it saved his life, but only just in time as the place where he stood was some twenty seconds later entirely demolished. The Opera House was completely destroyed, our HQ in the Castile demolished, and the whole of Valetta presented a sorry sight when the dust clouds lifted. But wanton and useless attacks on churches, prominent buildings, the Palace and inhabited areas were not sufficient for these German pilots. In the end they deliberately attacked even the hospitals. One German officer who had been taken prisoner and had been treated there proceeded to render great help in evacuating the wounded from the hospital wards. And even he was horrified by the deliberation with which the attacks were carried out.

By now, as an effective defensive force, there was no doubt that the RAF were spent. The AOC himself said: "If it were not for the soldiers we should be out of business." On eleven days in April they never took the air at all, and on many other days it was only for one raid in each day. It says much, therefore, for the gallantry of the pilots who went up against these insuperable odds that by their efforts they brought down fifty-six confirmed destroyed during that hectic month. Their gallantry was something which no one could help but admire. It was superb—as heroic as the Charge of the Light Brigade. It was unfortunate, therefore, that the tone of the BBC broadcasts and newspaper communiques painted such a false picture which tended locally to detract from that admiration. Daily announcements such as "Malta carries on under its umbrella of fighters" and "Malta's fighters cause great losses again to the enemy," although they may be stirring from an empire and propaganda point of view, were received with very different spirit in that beleaguered Island where the true position was to be seen every day. For some reason the AA Artillery were never given their full due during this time. Two only of many instances will serve to illustrate these remarks. On one day fourteen 'planes were destroyed, two by fighters and twelve by anti-aircraft artillery. The BBC version of this was "Our Spitfires and Hurricanes, assisted by the AA, destroyed fourteen 'planes over Malta". Finally, at the end of April, the AA had brought down a record total of one hundred and two enemy 'planes confirmed destroyed. This was reported in the Press as follows: "Malta's fighters have brought down fifty-six 'planes in their heroic battles for the safety of Malta." This was followed by a short description of the conditions under which they were operating. The last sentence of the paragraph stated: "The AA claim one hundred and two."

Now this was a gross injustice to the successes the guns had achieved. The implication of the word "claim" was bad enough as no single aircraft was counted as destroyed unless it was checked and cross checked and agreed by the RAF authorities also. This figure of one hundred and two by AA alone in one month was unapproached elsewhere over such a small area and should have been given "banner headlines." But where this policy was further mistaken was that some four thousand of Malta's sons were manning those guns, facing the heaviest weight of bomb attack ever then known, in conjunction and co-operation with their British comrades. Even as they fired bravely never counting the cost against the advancing hordes, they had only to look over their shoulder and see their own homes and villages being systematically destroyed. It was no wonder, therefore, that there were murmurings against the discrimination that seemed to be shown against them in the presentation of news from the mother country. It was unfortunate, as it caused the only tension that ever existed between the Services. How much happier was Lord Gort's message later to the authorities at home in which he stated that "for two long months the brunt of the battle was borne by the guns." However, early in May the RAF were at last able to be reinforced and to take the air in something like equality with the Luftwaffe. It was then that they gloriously earned every bit of the praise that was lavished upon them.

But during this time it was the Battle of the Guns. There was no gun position more bombed or in a more exposed area than that on Manoel Island. I remember once seeing an intensive attack put in against this gallant gun position which protected the submarine base. The bombs were dropped with great accuracy, and a thousand-pounder scored a direct hit on one of the guns. But even as it burst and the whole area seemed to be covered with black smoke I saw four red flashes burst through the haze. It was the last flash of the gun that was hit, but the other three carried on without cessation or hesitation, until the attack was over. That is only one instance, but of such was the gallantry of every gun position on the Island.

There are two others that I would like to mention here and now. One afternoon there was a very heavy attack on the Harbour area and some men of a Light Anti-Aircraft Regiment were enjoying a few hours relief in Valetta. During the attack a Light AA position a few hundred yards away from where they were standing was seen by them to be hit and suffer casualties. Without a moment's hesitation, although the gun belonged to another Regiment, they ran down to the position in charge of their Sergeant. The Sergeant told the NCO who had been commanding and was wounded, to hand over his gun and let him engage the next wave of bombers; the men meanwhile took the places of those who had been wounded. The Bombardier refused to hand over and the next wave of bombers was engaged under his direction. It was only after this when he was given an order by the Sergeant that he surrendered his position and went for treatment, while the gun remained in action throughout the rest of the raid.

The other instance concerns a concert party which was made up of well-known artistes on the amateur and professional stage in peace time, who were now all gunners. They got together and produced a really excellent high class programme with which they toured Artillery positions and by their efforts contributed largely to the maintenance of high morale everywhere. One day they were getting their props ready at a Heavy AA position and bombs began to fall. Some casualties occurred and these few men immediately dashed to the guns and took the place of the wounded for the remainder of the raid. When the raid was over they went straight back to the props, erected their stage, which they carried about on a horse-drawn cart, and gave their show as if nothing in the world had occurred.

But the losses of the Luftwaffe were proving heavy. Quite apart from those that we were definitely bringing down by the combined efforts of the fighters and the AA there were many more that we knew for certain would never get home and yet could not claim as no one actually saw them drop. In addition the number that must have returned badly damaged could not have failed to have been very great. In the afternoon of April 26th after two heavy raids by the Germans in the morning, the air alarm went for the usual evening raid. But this raid seemed to be much slower in building up and in its approach. Nick, who had been in the Control Room came out to find me and said "The RT is all in Italian", and sure enough, an Italian raid it proved. Five Italian bombers proceeded to cross the Island at an immense height, pursuing exactly the same tactics they had followed since the beginning of the war, and although bombs were falling the whole Island metaphorically put its hands on its hips and roared with laughter. The next few days the raids were all Italian. The Luftwaffe had called it off. Malta's defences, even though it should prove only a lull, sat back satisfied. It had been a battle of Titans and we had won the first round.

Throughout this book you will have read a great deal about the offensive tactics of the enemy. This is because in any air attack the bombers have the initiative, but now I would like to tell you of the methods that we used to combat these hordes. First of all, the man responsible to the Governor for the operation of all the artillery in the Island was the CRA. On his shoulders rested the heavy responsibilities and decisions that had to be taken, never more so than when the menace of ammunition shortage loomed up. He began to sense that there might be trouble in this direction in February and the Heavy AA were instructed not to engage fighter aircraft, but only to fire pointer rounds to show the position of the enemy to our fighters. Later on the restrictions which were applied in order to give rest, also served to economise further in ammunition. Geographical barrages were limited in mid-February to only three rounds per gun without a direct order to repeat. On the 10th April an order had to be issued only allowing fifty per cent of the Bofor positions to be in action at any one time, except those directly protecting ships unloading or specially sited for airfield defence. These we kept fully in action, and a system was evolved whereby our fighters could circle within their protective screen and land comparatively secure from the attentions of the marauding ME 109s and 110s. Ammunition restrictions were removed whenever a reinforcement of fighters was expected and re-imposed immediately they were safely on the ground. Finally, in mid-April, the position was becoming desperate and all the HAA and LAA were limited to fifteen rounds per gun per day, averaged out all over the Island. When one considers that fifteen rounds could be fired off by a Bofor in some seven seconds, it will be realised how drastic was the order and how carefully the targets had to be chosen before a single round was fired.

Under the CRA came the HAA Bde commanded by Brigadier Hire, who was responsible for all the technical planning and operation of the 3″, 3.7″ and 4.5″ guns. The LAA Bde was now commanded by Brigadier Woolley, who had succeeded Brigadier Sadler when the latter left to obtain command of an AA Bde at home which, curiously enough, became responsible for the AA defence of Dover, so he returned to the station he came from. Finally, for seaward defence there came the coast artillery under Brigadier White and for land attack there were the two Field Regiments, which were also administered by him, but under the operational command of HQ RA. Under the urgent representations made by the CRA the defencés of Malta had been vastly increased by the importation of a large number of 18 pounders for beach defence purposes. But it was in the AA world that our main strength lay and he had now built it up to the almost fantastic total of one hundred and twelve Heavy AA guns and one hundred and forty-four Light AA guns. Investigation proved that there was no point over Malta itself at which less than eighty Heavy AA guns could fire at one time, and the density of Light AA fire rose to proportionate heights in the vulnerable areas. This is a concentration that few pilots would care to face, particularly when reinforced by the guns of HM Ships, as often was the case. It was no wonder that the Luftwaffe cried quits.

But mere armament is not sufficient. The guns have got to be handled effectively. The standard method of engagement "height control" was used whenever possible, but different methods had to be employed when the Germans resorted to mass diving tactics. During the first year these had mainly been by means of Stukas which dived nearly vertically and so the geographical barrages over the actual target areas proved effective deterrants. But with the advent of the JU 88 and its long shallow dive other methods had to be adopted. Two of the more successful of these were the Chevron Barrage and the Xmas Barrage. The former was fired in the form of a V, like a Lance Corporal's stripes, across the line of descent. By a series of intricate adjustments, each barrage was made in the form of a hexagon, so that the two arms of the hexagon nearest to the line of approach could be fired. The height could be varied at will. To avoid this barrage laterally the bombers would have to go out of their course and so would miss the target. But it was shallow in depth and they soon discovered that they could go over it, or under it, and another means had to be devised. Brigadier Hire and his Staff Officers got down to it on Christmas Eve (we think with the aid of a whisky bottle) and finally came up to HQ RA with the suggestion of the Xmas Barrage, which the CRA immediately appreciated would prove effective. This was a barrage fired by the five Heavy AA Regiments in the form of a five on a dice, forming an X in the sky. This gave greater density and very soon proved its efficacy. The Xmas spirit had triumphed · and gave its name to the barrage. Look-outs were stationed round the Island with excellent communications to the main operations room, so that in addition to the radio location information, visual running commentaries could be given to aid the orders to the guns when gun operations room were controlling the fire centrally. Purists in the AA world will shudder at these combinations of barrages, but in the actual test of war they proved themselves more than efficient against the tremendous density of attack that we endured. Lastly, for attacks on gun positions the rule was "keep firing all the time and he won't be able to aim so well". This rule was never broken and the result was that our casualties were quite remarkably light when the scale of attack is taken into consideration.

The Light AA were faced with yet another problem—the problem of dust. No sooner did the Heavy AA guns open up, or the first bombs fall, than the dust cloud immediately sprang up, blinding everyone and everything. It soon became obvious that if all the guns were close to the target area they would be useless, as they could not see the attacking 'planes. And so they were deployed in two rings, an inner ring as close to the aerodrome as possible, without becoming immediately involved in the dust, and an outer ring which, having more time to adjust its fire, could be regarded as the killing ring. Of their gallantry I have already written, and their contribution to the April total of one hundred and two was almost exactly half, which was a reward for the devoted way in which they handled their guns. .

Finally it must not be thought that the rest of the Garrison were standing by watching this battle as interested spectators. A very large proportion of the Army were employed in making dispersal areas and pens for aircraft on the aerodromes. The work was urgent and vital and was kept up night and day, air-raids or no air-raids, with little or no protection for the men. Infantry, Field and Defence Artillery all co-operated and in two months over three hundred aeroplane pens and twenty seven miles of dispersal areas were made. Anyone who knows Malta rock will appreciate the magnitude of that effort. But that was not all. Craters on runways had to be filled in, houses and billets repaired, stores rescued from bombed buildings, and constant efforts had to be made to discover new accommodation for those suddenly rendered homeless. The soldiers were particularly noted for their help to the ARP Department and the civil population, and whenever there was any work to be done, like digging persons out from under piles of debris, they were always among the first to take off their coats and get down to it. The ordinary comforts of life, such as water, light and gas were constantly being put out of action and the Army helped to put them right. Also, they assisted in clearing away the debris. It was a case of everyone helping his neighbour and right well was the job done.

But still there remains one person whose part in this great battle against the Axis has not yet been fully revealed and with whose name the heroic Island's defence will always be associated. General Sir William Dobbie (he had received his knighthood since becoming Governor), was the man upon whose shoulders rested the final decisions on the recommendations made to him by his Service Chiefs. It was he who was ultimately responsible for the successful defence of Malta. Not only had he got to weigh up the pros and cons of the military, naval and air aspects of each changing situation, but upon him also was the added burden of the welfare and well-being of the very vast civilian element with all its intricate politics. It was a burden which was almost more than human endurance should be asked to bear. But General Dobbie was a man who did not consider for one moment that such responsibilities were to be solved by human endeavor alone. He has publicly stated, and everyone who knows him well will believe it, that in his trials and tribulations he turned to God for his inspiration and for his help, and from Him he derived the necessary strength and wisdom.

Right from the very beginning this Governor had made himself a hero in the eyes of his people. It was he who had first taken a strong line against the bombastic threats from sixty miles away. It was shortly after his arrival that an adequate garrison began to be built up in Malta. It was at his insistence that defence works were erected throughout the Island and preparations made to provide protection for the inhabitants against inevitable air attack. When war was finally declared, it was his broadcast, in which he committed himself, the garrison, and the whole Island to the mercy of God, confident that, whatever trials would have to be endured, right would eventually triumph with His aid, which endeared him finally and for all time in the hearts and equally simple faiths of the Maltese. Wherever the battle was at its height there was the Governor to be seen. His courage was tremendous. He seemed oblivious of falling bombs or the heavy bits of AA splinters that came hurtling out of the sky. If he was not there during the raid it was only a matter of moments before His Excellency was present on the scene of each major tragedy, doing all he could to give sympathetic help to the victims and relatives and to ensure that practical aid was immediately forthcoming. A man in his position, Governor of a lonely Island in the middle of a sea that was for all intents and purposes hostile territory, might have been forgiven if his outlook had

Lt-Gen Sir William Dobbie, Governor and Commander-in-Chief watches a parade of Malta University Officer Cadets in company with Brig (later Maj-Gen) C. T. Beckett, CRA Malta, Professor Galea, Vice-Chancellor of the University, Maj Fleetwood, Commandant of the Training Depot, and in rear Brig Gatt and the author.

been bounded entirely by the shores of the little area that it was his duty to defend. But General Dobbie constantly bore in mind the fact that Malta merely formed part of a pattern. Her retention was essential to the strategy of the battles in the Middle East, but at the same time the mother country's needs were great also. So before he ever sanctioned the requests for convoys to be despatched to Malta replete with all the varied assortments of supplies so necessary for an island that was utterly non-selfsufficient, he weighed his request in the balance against the well-known difficulties of production and shortages of shipping that were faced by the allies as a whole. Perhaps if convoys could have been more frequent during those months when we only had the Italians to contend with our supply anxieties might not have been so great. On the other hand, before the battles started the Island had reserves of stocks for many months and the severity of the blockade could hardly have been foreseen. Certainly there were moments when the Island's resources nearly gave out. One thing is certain, General Dobbie recognised the importance of Malta, and he vowed that its defence would be sure. It must have been of great comfort to him when finally he laid down his charge to know that the Island still stood firm and resolute and that the Luftwaffe had confessed their failure after having thrown their massed might into the battle. Therein lay the justification of all that he had done.

But the anxieties of those months and years of constant responsibility was bound to tell. Those who saw him during the months of March and April were worried by the obvious signs of strain that he was revealing. Maybe it was the fall of Singapore that had caused him a very real set-back. He was like so many others in believing that our Far East fortress was impregnable and he had openly expressed that opinion. As GOC Malaya some years before it was he who had been responsible for erecting those magnificent defences against seaward attack. The loss of this far eastern naval base in a matter of days was bound to affect anyone so closely connected with its past glory and even more so a man who was then responsible for the maintenance in safety of Britain's Mediterranean naval base. We were not to know at that time that he was a sick man physically and that within a few days of his return to England he was to be admitted to hospital for an urgent operation. It was not like General Dobbie to say anything about his own physical ailments while the safety of the Island was at stake.

One day at the end of April I met Lady Dobbie and her daughter Sybil photographing the wreckage of the Palace in

Valetta. She told me that they would be leaving for home . quite shortly but that no official announcement could yet be given. One realised the shock with which it would be received by the inhabitants of the Island to whom "Dobbie of Malta" with his straightforward faith in God had become a figurehead to whom they looked for strength and inspiration for their defence. As they stood near the landing stage in Marza Scirocco Bay waiting for the aeroplane to take him to England, General Sir William Dobbie, if it was in him to show pride of any kind, could look round that small Island of which he had been Governor for so long with a thrill of pride in his achievement. Under him it had stood up to attack from the sea and to the heaviest onslaught from the air yet known. That inspired gesture at the crux of the April battle—the personal award by His Majesty The King of The George Cross—had been earned under his governorship even though it fell to his successor to present it to the Island. Under him the morale of the inhabitants had never wavered for one instant, and under his guidance Malta had weathered the full fury of the storm and was even now on the threshold of victory.

CHAPTER IX

Climax

The sorrow that was evinced by all at the loss of their gallant Governor was only equalled by the satisfaction with which the news was received that Lord Gort, the Governor of Gibraltar, was to be transferred to Malta as the new Commander-in-Chief. His very arrival was a thrill in itself. He came by flying boat in the early hours of darkness and landed in, Marza Scirocco Bay just as an air-raid was commencing. All the civil dignitaries were ready to receive him and to swear him in as Governor. During the actual ceremony a bomb fell only some thirty yards from the little hut in which he was taking the oath of allegiance. Maybe it was lack of practice, but more probably it was personal courage that left the new Governor standing upright while everyone else was prostrate on the ground. This story achieved a rapid and wide circulation in the Island and added lustre, if lustre was needed, to the fame of the new Governor. It must be confessed that at this moment Malta was at the crisis in its fortunes. The Luftwaffe had called off the attack, but there were no signs of its departure from its Sicilian bases. There were even the first signs of a build-up in landing craft and stores such as would precede an invasion. Lord Gort realised that the guns, particularly with their limited supplies of ammunition, could not hold out indefinitely against the resources of the Axis. But in addition to the shortage of ammunition there was a yet more serious shortage—the lack of food for the children of the Island. And also he appreciated that if Malta was to be saved she had got to be able to compete on almost equal terms with the Luftwaffe in the air.

I have called this chapter the "climax" and I make no apology for so doing. In length of engagement this was a short battle compared with the long drawn out struggles of the months before, but in fierceness it far out-did its predecessors and proved decisive in saving the Island from military disaster. There can perhaps have been no finer example of the need for inter Service co-operation than was provided by the defence of Malta. An adequate AA defence was necessary before fighters from the

RAF could be based on the Island. In those days of short-range fighters it took a large scale naval operation before those little aeroplanes could take their part in the battle. Their very presence in Malta was only due—like the guns—to the gallantry of the Navy and the Merchant Navy. In their turn, under their protection, His Majesty's Ships, and most gallant of all, His Majesty's Submarines, were able to operate for long periods at a time. And so it will be seen how completely inter-dependent all the Services were on each other. But in such an isolated and beleaguered fortress there still remains the fourth aspect before the defences can be said to be facing foursquare to the aggressor. It would not have been possible for any of these Services to operate successfully without the goodwill, support and self-sacrifice of the civilian population. Of this last there will be much more to say later on. For the time being the story of the epic of HMS Welshman will concern only the three Services, but will provide the finest example of co-operation that could ever be devised.

One of the first acts of His Excellency the Governor after his arrival was to set up a Conference at which all the heads of his Services could meet and discuss their plans of defence. Under his firm leadership priorities were decided and the efforts of all were directed towards the common good. The plan for the immediate relief of the garrison and its shortages of ammunition for the guns, and milk for the children, was evolved at this conference and carried through with the complete co-operation of all ranks of all Services. HMS Welshman, a fast mine-laying cruiser, was to make a dash at top speed through "bomb alley", that stretch of the Western Mediterranean from Gibraltar to Malta that was practically entirely dominated by the Axis. It was hoped that with her great speed of nearly forty knots she might be able to slip through the most dangerous part of the journey past Pantalleria during the hours of darkness. Then her greatest trials would be from attack from the air where again her great speed would be of assistance to her in dodging the salvoes of bombs and in cutting down the time which the enemy would have for mounting new attacks if the early ones failed. But it was useless to expect any ship to carry out such a project alone and unaided. She had to be protected from the skies and so a vast naval operation was planned whereby some sixty-five Spitfires could be flown off the decks of HMS Eagle and the US aircraft carrier Wasp sufficiently near to Malta to ensure their safe arrival in the Island. With vivid memories of what had happened in the past when reinforcements of fighters had landed and then been largely destroyed on the ground, the task of making all the preparations for their reception and safety fell to the Army. Miles of runway were constructed and aeroplane pens sprang up overnight as a result of the honest toil and sweat of the Manchesters, Buffs, West Kents, Devons, Dorsets and Hampshires soldiery to mention only some of the battalions taking part. But not even the maintenance crews for such a large number of fighters existed in Malta. Thomas Atkins was therefore detailed to take over the servicing of aeroplanes and many ground staffs consisted of nothing but soldiers from the infantry, supervised by technical NCOs of the RAF. The AA prepared the most concentrated barrages that had ever been devised for the safety of HMS Welshman when she reached dock and was unloading her precious supplies. When eventually it was fired into the sky it appeared to be almost a solid cone of metal. Similar powerful barrages were provided for the protection of each aerodrome in the event of a direct attack upon it. All ammunition restrictions were lifted so that the maximum effort of the anti-aircraft would be available.

The tenseness in the Island as the day approached could almost be felt. Few people knew the details of the plan, but there was hardly a single soul that did not realise that something big was afoot. On 9th May the Spitfires took off from their aircraft carriers which had been heavily escorted by major units of the British battle fleet. All sixty-five of them flew direct to Malta, only one failing to reach the Island. The remainder all landed on the airfields to which they had been directed before their take-off. Hal Far aerodrome had been enlarged for this purpose. Ta Kali aerodrome had had its dispersal areas spread to an unrecognisable degree and more aircraft pens had been built not only on Luqa aerodrome but on the strip leading past Safi down to Hal Far. As each aeroplane began its taxiing run along its selected aerodrome after landing it saw in front of it a motor-cyclist bearing a number. These motor-cyclists were mainly members of the Field and Defence Artillery. The pilot had been directed to follow the motor-cyclist bearing his number who would lead him into the correct pen. No sooner were they parked inside the pen than the pilot was removed and a gang of soldiers and airforce personnel set about preparing the aeroplane for action while the new pilot waited actually in the pen until the moment for action was at hand. It was these soldiers who filled up the tanks with petrol, loaded the ammunition belts with the cannon shells, fitted the guns onto the 'planes and, under the supervision of their RAF Instructors, did the other hundred and one odd jobs of maintenance so essential for the safety of any aircraft. Other members of the Field Artillery were standing by in the dockyard area ready to launch a smoke screen over the Harbour as soon as an attack became iminent. Still others, both of the Artillery and the Infantry, were occupied in unloading the boxes of stores and in driving them away in their military transport to the selected depots.

The whole operation went as smoothly as clockwork. Kesselring, sitting some sixty or seventy miles away in the island of Sicily had noticed from his radar reports the arrival of sixty aircraft in Malta. And so he proceeded to apply the same tactics that he had used so successfully on previous occasions. A massed raid was prepared and finally launched. But this time he had not reckoned on the increased maintenance facilities for the RAF, such as had been provided by the military. Instead of a matter of twenty-four hours to prepare these 'planes for combat as had been thought by the RAF to be necessary, the 'planes were ready for action in many cases in twenty minutes and in one case it is said that it only took six minutes before the pilot was ready to fly off the ground in his completely prepared Spitfire. Kesselring's hordes swept up into the skies and began to make their way towards their familiar target. But this time, for the first time in the history of Malta, the RAF met the enemy on equal terms. Ta Kali was the main objective of the Huns and there was no doubt that they got the shock of their lives when these famous fighters came at them from all directions on their approach to the target. Dozens of unexploded bombs were dropped that day, which alone testifies to the unpreparedness of the German crews in that they did not even wait to charge the bombs before letting them go in the face of the onslaught that met them. It was a magnificent sight. The surrounding sea seemed to be constantly throwing up white spumes of spray as yet another enemy 'plane took its last plunge to destruction. Soldiers, sailors and civilians alike were ecstatic in their praise of the RAF victories and the anti-aircraft gunners themselves, for so long the bulwark of Malta's defence, yielded to none in their admiration of the boys in blue.

It is probable that till a few hours later the Germans had no inkling of the approach of HMS Welshman. All that night she was steaming full speed through the Mediterranean darkness on her never-to-be-forgotten dash to the Grand Harbour. Early next morning, however, there was no doubt that they knew of her presence. She tied up safely in harbour and almost before she had been properly secured to her moorings her decks were a swarming mass of military unloading her cargo of ammunition and powdered milk. The warning went, and the smoke screen began to wreathe its vapouring trails over the ship. Very soon it became a dense mass so that everything in the area of French Creek became obscured. The Germans approached with great gallantry and in great force. They even braved the dangers of that flaming cone of metal, the greatest concentrated barrage of AA Artillery ever known. Meanwhile the fighters had been circling round just on the outskirts of the barrage and were doing great slaughter amongst the attacking bombers. Those that survived the barrage then became an easy prey for any of our fighters that happened to be near them as they wobbled away in a damaged condition. But the "Welshman" and its cargo were a prize that the Germans could not afford to ignore. They tried again and again. They even persuaded the Italians to do one of their high flying raids, but gallant HMS Welshman remained unscathed to the end and at seven o'clock that night after exactly twelve hours in port she left on schedule, having fulfilled her task of bringing the desperately needed ammunition for the Light AA guns and powdered milk for the civilians. Not only had her venture brought actual relief to the Island but her arrival had incited the Luftwaffe to take the air in force and to suffer the most resounding defeat it had yet sustained in its history in the Mediterranean. Some one hundred and one 'planes during those thirty-six hours were either confirmed brought down or damaged to such a pitch that it would have been impossible for them to struggle home. It was the rapier thrust that comes at the end of a long and tiring battle with a mad bull in the bull-ring and it was decisive. It was more than the Luftwaffe could stomach after the losses it had sustained during the month of April. Except for one very brief return, massed raiding against Malta was to be a thing of the past from that day on and the Germans admitted it themselves when in a broadcast they said darkly "Malta can be reduced by other means".

CHAPTER X

Second Interval

After all the hurly burly and strain of the earlier months of the year and in particular that historic week-end, the calm that reigned over Malta came as a welcome relief. It was almost difficult to believe that war had been so intimate a part of our lives. Malta in May is perhaps almost at its best. The beautiful green of the countryside is only just beginning to turn to golden and the colours of the fields contrast vividly with the bright exuberance of the oleanders lining the roads. The sky is as blue as only a picture postcard of the Mediterranean could rival. The sun beats down on the beaches and the sea laps the coasts in little ripples, giving to the whole Island a setting of quiet and peace. What a contrast that formed to the previous month of that year of 1942. No longer did we look up into the skies and see hordes of aeroplanes with black crosses on them diving down to sow death and destruction on garrison and inhabitants alike. There was time now for everybody in turn to take a little rest from their labours and get away for brief hours from the scenes of desolation and devastation that were their usual surroundings.

It was as I was lying out in the Calderon's garden one afternoon that I looked back on all the eventful happenings that we had so recently gone through. If I quote my own experiences it is only because I am more familiar with them than with anybody else's. There was no difference in the events that happened to me from those that were the common lot of all in the Island. In fact I had been luckier than some. I had not yet been dug out from under debris nor had I suffered any calamitous loss in the way of kit or furniture. The original flat that I occupied had been totally destroyed by a mine but a couple of weeks after I had left it. By then I had moved to another overlooking the submarine base and, in fact, about midway between it and the Grand Harbour. For some reason, although bombs fell all around, this one building seemed to bear a charmed existence, but eventually, although it stood up it became too draughty to endure. From my bed I could not only see into the kitchen next door, but through that into the dining-room, so large were the cracks in the walls. It was without the slightest difficulty that, through another crack, I watched the harbour defence searchlights sweeping the seas at night. The front door was blown off its hinges on almost every occasion that a bomb dropped on Manoel Island (which was nearly daily), and I eventually decided that the time had come when a move to a more solid building was indicated. It was about the time that I reached this decision that the front half of our Mess, which used to be the Mess of the Royal Malta Artillery, was destroyed by a bomb, just after lunch one day. We reorganised the place and managed to fit ourselves into the back half, but that did not satisfy the Hun, and three days later he destroyed that too. Almost coincident with this latter destruction came the raid on the Castile which wrecked every one of our offices, and so we were forced to devise a makeshift Mess and offices in the bowels of the earth, in which were located the HQ of Malta Command. This troglodyte existence proved too much for all our tempers, and it was unanimously voted that we must return to fresh air and freedom for thought. And so another building was prepared for our Mess, but no sooner was it ready than the Hun promptly destroyed that too.

By now Valetta was just a shambles. I had moved my flat to share with Fish, of whom I have previously written, and our half of the house still remains to this day, but it was the first building in South Street that was in any way habitable. Kingsway, principle street of Valetta, was just one mass of ruins and shattered shops, crowned at its entrance by the pathetic wreckage of the famous Opera House. Everywhere one looked one could see nothing but desolation and rubble. In particular was this so if one walked on to the top of the ramparts and looked down on some of the streets. It was then that one realised the extent of the damage. Malta's buildings are made of very solid blocks of stone and it takes a direct hit to destroy a house. The traveller arriving in Valetta might, at first, think that the damage was comparatively slight, but let him just walk to one high vantage point and look down and he will see that almost every building is nothing but an empty shell. That alone will show the intensity of the bombing. It was estimated at one time that there were a million five hundred thousand tons of debris in Valetta and Floriana alone. In the whole Island over fifteen thousand buildings had been destroyed, amongst them seventy churches, eighteen convents or monasteries, twenty-two schools, eight hospitals, ten theatres—but the list is endless. In the crowded areas of Floriana, Senglea and Valetta over 75 per cent of the buildings were uninhabitable. In one month alone, April, seven thousand tons of bombs had rained down on Britain's sea-

The scene inside St John's Cathedral during the Requiem
Mass for Cardinal Hinsley, celebrated by Archbishop
Caruana. Note the sandbags protecting the altar.

girt sentinel of the Mediterranean. There may have been some truth in the jest that "During the month of April, Malta had six all-clears, one of which lasted for thirty-five minutes."

With all these figures it will be realised how hopeless it was to seek for further accommodation for offices and Messes in that devastated area. And so the CRA gave orders for HQ RA to move. We were lucky in that there was a Convent, St. Agatha's Convent, in Rabat which was being used for the detention of that infinitesimal minority who favoured the Italians. Some three or four weeks before our move took place the most truculent of these had been sent out of the Island, their departure being accelerated by a strong decision on the part of General Dobbie. One of them had questioned the legality of this decision, but it would have been better for him if he had acquiesced. He was allowed to remain behind as a test case and the very next day after the others had sailed, a German bomb, landing at the entrance to St. Agatha's Convent, removed him and all necessity for an enquiry into the legality of his intended expulsion. The remaining inhabitants of the convent were not considered sufficiently rabid in their views to be detained any longer, and so we took up our residence there, greatly assisted by the help that was given us by the former Commandant of the Internees Camp, my old friend Walter Bonello.

One might well ask, with all this widespread destruction, whether the casualties in the island had been enormous? It was said that one in every seventy of the population had been a casualty of some kind, but the number of killed was very small in comparison with the scale of attack. The deep shelters had proved the salvation of the civilian population. In fact, it may be of interest to note that by midsummer of 1942 the number of enemy airmen killed or captured over Malta was almost exactly double the fatal civilian casualties. But although the casualties were light relationships in the island are so close that very great distress was caused by them, although the courage with which these losses were faced was something to be wondered at. One memory that I shall never be able to efface was that of a very young and very pretty wife staying with her husband under the kindly and sympathetic protection of Sir William and Lady Dobbie at the Palace. From her quiet demeanour and lack of any outward demonstration of grief in public, no one would have guessed that only a few days before she had lost her baby in the shelter that they had had specially constructed and to which they had sent the child and nurse for protection when the raid began. It was the kind of bravery that gave to everyone who met them a catch in the throat because there was not a soul who did not know how great was their private sorrow.

The children of Malta seemed quite undaunted by all that had occurred. One could not fail to notice their bright smiles and cheerful demeanour. Walking down Kingsway one had to return so many salutes from service men (saluting in Malta was always exemplary) that it might have been less tiring to emulate Moses during the battle and keep one's arm permanently in the saluting position. But apart from them there still remained the youngsters. Every child in Malta seemed to take a special pride in saluting every officer who passed. As a military car approached they would dash from whatever they were doing to line the route and greet the occupants with the smartest of smart salutes. Everybody made a point of returning them most punctiliously and then they would break off with their little faces wreathed in smiles. Not only in the open but from casement windows, inside rock shelters, and from behind mountains of debris the youth of Malta, both male and female, used to vie with each other in paying the proper compliments. They were very remarkable these children. They had seen their homes destroyed, their playthings shattered, and they certainly knew what hunger was. They lived a dark and gloomy existence in communal shelters where they could not laugh or play for fear of disturbing everyone else. The streets with their jumbled masses of masonry were their sole playground and then only when there were no bombers overhead. Their deep sense of religion and the feeling of security and trust engendered in them from their earliest days by the sight of their precious churches and images had been rudely shattered by the vandal Hun. All these things and more they had had to endure and yet they still turned to greet the passers by with laughing faces, smiling eyes and exemplary salutes. Nobody who ever saw them or ever had the privilege of knowing them could deny that it was the children themselves who should have been saluted first.

But, of course, civilian damage was not all that occurred during these testing times. Deliberate attacks against gun positions had been part of the German tactics and had been ruthlessly carried out. It was only the bravery of the gun detachments that saved the losses to men and equipment from becoming very heavy. On not one single occasion did a gun detachment take cover against the diving 'planes. In every case the attacker was met with every weapon that was at the disposal of the defender. As a result, the percentage of guns that were destroyed in the Island was very small. But it would have been larger if it had not been for the heroic work that was carried out by Leslie Tyler who was the ADME during these times. No job was too big for him to tackle, from repairing a practically pulverised gun in twenty-four hours to the production of some new sort of platform upon which an undamaged piece could be mounted. He, and those under him, worked, some said, for thirty-six hours out of twenty-four, using all their skill and ingenuity in repairs and improvisations. Without any of the usual resources and assemblies that the REME have at their disposal, he had worked miracles in workshops that had been blitzed, and in gun positions that were being attacked. The gunners owed a lot to him and when he received his reward in the form of an OBE the sincerest congratulations that he received emanated from our ranks.

Leslie Tyler's family had meanwhile been braving all these attacks and living in the area of St. Julians. This residential part of the Sliema side of the harbours had become a sort of English Colony and the thirsty and weary officer passing through there on his way from one duty to another was always sure of a kindly welcome and refreshment from one or other of the residents. Situated in the middle of St. Julians was "Careel" a house which offered unlimited hospitality to all, presided over by Colonel Ede, the Defence Security Officer of the Island and "C" his charming wife. There was some quality about the atmosphere at "Careel" that placed it in a class entirely of its own. Perhaps it was the lawn on which one could have tea brought out; maybe it was the tennis court where so many of us disported ourselves; perhaps it was the impeccable taste of the furnishings of all the rooms. Whatever it was Bertram and "C" were responsible for it and I always had a feeling when I was there that I had stepped into another world, a peaceful world reminiscent of English gardens, Devonshire cream and crumpets, all of which were unknown in Malta. It only took a few hours in the pleasant company of the Edes to refresh one for a return to the stark realities of life in the rest of Malta.

It was from "C" Ede that I first heard tell that the building of the Malta Amateur Dramatic Club had been destroyed. I rushed down to Valetta to see if this dreadful rumour was true. Alas, it was so. In the very last attack made on Valetta a bomb had scored a direct hit on its premises. I stood on the other side of South Street and looked up, recalling many memories that were associated with those derelict walls. I felt that the MADC had stood for something in all these troubles and had tried in its own small way to lighten the burden that was being borne by everyone. I rang up K and told her the sad news. To K and Ella the MADC had been practically their home for many years. They knew every single prop, every book, every piece of furniture and every roll of scenery, so that for them I knew its loss would be a very real sorrow. At tea a few days later at their house in Rabat, K asked if it would not be possible for a small memorial for the MADC to be written and circulated to all its members. I mentioned the idea to Mabel Strickland, who immediately, with her usual generosity, said: "You write it and I'll print it in 'The Times of Malta'". So here it is for all those members outside the island, to whom copies were either never sent or have foundered on the way.

"THE WORLD'S A STAGE"
A TRIBUTE TO THE MALTA AMATEUR DRAMATIC CLUB
(Published in the "Sunday Times" of Malta 24th May 1942)

It is curious how pathetic a bombed building looks and what appeal it makes to the sentimental inclinations of all who knew it in its pristine state. A building that has just been a building to its users so long as it remained erect and serviceable becomes a temple of memories, suddenly assuming a mantle of pathos when its life has been drastically cut short by a bomb. It looks so desolate. Maybe one wall still remains intact and on it a picture is hanging all awry. Perhaps a table or a chair are balanced precariously across a beam. Sometimes just the outside wall has been sheered away, leaving a stage setting of real life. The casual passer-by may even feel embarrassed as he glimpses the treasured possessions and intimate touches of a home now ruthlessly exposed to view. For such are scenes of reality and not settings for dramas of synthetic life.

Even so, standing outside the ruined remnants of what for so many had been the home of amateur drama in Malta and surveying the last set, albeit an involuntary one, that would ever be staged in those premises, a host of memories and recollections—some personal and some by repute—came thronging into mind. Desolation reigned supreme but above the pile of tumbled masonry there could still be seen the green room cupboards, a glimpse of the property room and some of the bits and pieces of furniture that for so long had fulfilled so many roles at rehearsals. One and all held out a promise that the spirit would never die but would rise again one day like a Phoenix from the ashes.

One pillar still stood, recalling to mind a performance of "Macbeth" on an English school stage by the Ben Greet Players. There was a pillar on that stage too, and Macduff's advancing army was presented by two members of the cast going round and round that pillar into the wings and out again until it seemed they must faint through dizziness. "Macbeth" recalled Banquo's ghost and with that thought, ghosts of memory walked across from behind that pillar to the gaping void that once had been a stage. Like Macduff's army came the wraiths of all those members to whom the club had opened wide its doors and for whom it had served for so long as a bond of friendship, both here and in other climes, and as a link across the oceans and the years. There were others too; was that the adorable Lilian Gish who had proved as demure and self-effacing in private as she is glamorous and compelling in public? Was one Mr. Noel Coward who had been so intrigued by the capacity of that little stage when he was in Malta, and another Lord Louis Mountbatten who had dropped in to attend some of the war-time rehearsals? And after them came Dame Sybil Thorndike and Mr. Lewis Casson, the Old Vic Company and the Dublin Gate Players, Miss Sybil Arundale and Mr. Robert Flemyng, who witnessed the part he had created and played for over 1,000 performances in London in the last production the Club ever gave at the Opera House. All of these and many others had entered those precincts and now their shadow-selves flitted across the scene.

What other memories? Days and evenings of discussion on the selection of the next play; thrills of excitement as suddenly out of the seemingly impenetrable chaos of rehearsal a scene took shape and became a live thing in which one could believe; moments of despair as one bit of business was rehearsed again and again to no apparent avail; flashes of temperament instantly curbed because friendship was the underlying principle of the club; stage romances blossoming into real romances; new friendships and fresh loyalties all being welded under its aegis; a sanctuary in war-time to which one could escape from the strain of battle to spend a brief hour in another world of pleasant make-believe; the delight of old members who returned to Malta to find rehearsals in progress; a broadcast tribute by the BBC to the contribution the club had made to achieving normality amid all the topsy-turvydom of the times; lastly, and sufficient reward in itself, a memory of a sea of laughing faces and clapping hands of friends packed into the tiny auditorium after they had been transported for a couple of hours to a land of smiles, far from the eternal theme of war.

The Club had contributed its quota to the war. Concert parties fostered by it and composed almost entirely of its members toured the Island from the commencement of hostilities, giving performances to troops on their positions, changing costumes in lorries or in tents or wherever some privacy from the outside world could be obtained. No privacy within those screens—

greasepaint, costumes, suitcases, wigs and travelling clothes were inextricably mingled together as changes of scene and dress were made. Then transport difficulties became too great. What next? The Club was determined to carry on. The usual venue of the Opera House was now taken over for more important purposes and so the tiny Club rehearsal stage was used, the club rooms converted into an auditorium, time for rehearsals snatched whenever performers could leave their duties, airraids made no difference and two plays were each successfully produced for a number of performances. Others were attempted. The spirit was ever willing but the difficulties were always great and often insuperable.

It had deserved a better fate than this wanton destruction. It had stood till the last attack on Valetta in April 1942, representative of all the principles for which this war is being waged—the right to free speech, liberty of thought and untrammelled laughter. And now, along with many other more beautiful, more famous and more hallowed buildings, it had finally been struck down. Its loss will be felt by many. Never again will members stream up those dark and smelly stairs, so reminiscent of all stage doors. Never again will rehearsals be conducted to the clink of bottles being washed and sorted in the wine firm on the floor below or to an anxious secretary's warning cry of "8d. a unit" as those footlights burnt overlong. Never again will the committee sit in judgement in those rooms while nervous newcomers display their talents on that tiny stage. But the spirit of the drama will survive all that a ruthless enemy can do and with it, as surely as dawn succeeds night, will rise again a new, and perhaps a better, Malta Amateur Dramatic Club.

Chapter XI

Act III

The third act of the drama of Malta is the most long drawn out of all but at the same time it is one whose description may take the least space. Starvation and siege—for such were the "other means" that the Axis now decided to employ—are not pleasant subjects nor can one do full justiçe to all their horrors and effects in describing them in pages which take merely a matter of minutes to read. It is their cumulative effect, the gradual loss of brightness in the eye, the loss of condition in the animals, the lack of spirits in the children and the eventual indifference as to what may happen next that become in the end the most telling aspects of this form of warfare.

If the story of HMS Welshman was one which more intimately concerned the Services, it was now that it became the turn of the civilians to bear an even greater burden in the combined resistance against the enemy. Lord Gort appreciated immediately on his arrival that Malta would have to be prepared to stand some months of siege. Probably even he at that time did not envisage the length of time which she would have to endure, as in May the retreat of the British Armies in Libya to the Alamein Line had not yet taken place. Tobruk was ours too and although the Eastern Mediterranean was dangerous for the passage of a convoy, yet if only the Luftwaffe could by some means be kept in subjection for a matter of two or three days the chances of running one to Malta were not impossible. But with the retreat beyond the borders of Egypt almost back to the Nile, Malta's position began to look hopeless. The Governor however had been very wise. He had not gambled on any future successes of the British Armies. Ruthlessly he instituted rationing on a scale that had never before been experienced in an Allied Country unoccupied by the enemy. Food shops were closed down. It became impossible even to buy a cup of coffee in a restaurant. Every single item was rationed down to fractions of an ounce. Foremost of all in this drastic rationing scheme came His Excellency and his staff. He gave orders that his household would exist on civilian rations which were infinitesimal compared even with the meagre rations allowed for the Army. Further than this, he abandoned his car and was to be seen even on the hottest days proceeding to The Council of Government in Valetta mounted on his bicycle. For many months the civilian population lived on very little more than air and determination. At one time, and for a considerable period, the meat ration was one half-pound tin of bully-beef per person per month. There were no potatoes in the Island as the crop had failed. All the flour was requisitioned and controlled by the Government for the making of bread. The fats ration was only a matter of ounces per fortnight and the sugar ration for the same period was not much more than one would normally put in a large cup of tea. Milk was cut down to a minute quantity each day with just a small increase for the children who were also given a special issue of a tiny morsel of chocolate each twice a month. One family that I knew well in Malta told me that for a fortnight after this rationing was instituted their maid had solemnly come into the sitting room and announced that dinner was served. The family had then moved to the dining room where they found one piece of dry toast each. This was their supper. After fourteen days of this they concluded that the ceremony could be dispensed with and the toast brought into the sitting room. If they even had the food there came the difficulty of cooking it. The fuel allowance was one quarter of a gallon of kerosene per head per month and even that allowance was scaled down slightly in the case of families of four or over. When one remembers that throughout the Island the gas had been destroyed and that the electricity was cut off for many weeks and then only given to the vital installations, it will be realised what a strain the housewife had to face in deciding how best to use that meagre ration as she tackled the problems of cooking, washing-up and bathing.

There was no doubt whatever that the civilians lived in a state of perpetual hunger during those months, although the diet was just sufficient to keep body and soul together. Food experts came out from England and did all that they could to make the most of anything that they were given, and the Army too had to face the severest reduction in rations. It has been stated that the Garrison was put on to half rations, but most of us who were there would regard that as an optimistic estimate of the situation. The military personnel were given slightly less bread each day, some eight ounces, than civilians, whose staple diet it is, but their ration of meat and fats was higher. This was rightly so as they had long and arduous labours to perform. Even so, one quarter of a pound of bully beef per day shared out between four meals cannot be described as very satisfying. It was the monotony of the food, the constant bully beef and the lack of any flour to make pastries or scones, and of potatoes to make cottage pies that became hard to bear. But there is no doubt that if one has to choose one single substance to live on for any length of time bully beef is probably better than any other. It can be handled in a variety of ways. I think we know them all now. The rations for the Army were obviously not sufficient to allow full training and full work to be performed so a compulsory rest hour was introduced into the routine each day. PT was abolished and the cross-country runs and long training marches were suspended. These last two had been the particular institutions of General Beak on his arrival. In order to set a good example to all the troops, he took part in them himself, and it is said that on his first run he stopped to ask a military policeman where the route went, only to receive the reply, "Can't you follow the —— flags?"

Shortly after the triumphant episode of HMS Welshman's safe arrival and departure, Air Vice Marshal Hugh Pugh Lloyd relinquished the appointment of Air Officer Commanding. During his tenure of office he had undoubtedly converted Malta into an offensive base that for long had proved a running sore in the Axis side. The nightly bomber sorties over Benghazi, Tripoli and Sicily had gone on almost uninterruptedly throughout the summer months of 1941 until the darkest days of the attacks in 1942. Swordfish aircraft of the fleet air arm operating under his control had sallied forth consistently in the first quarter of each moon to attack the enemy convoys with startling success. Photographic aircraft had roamed far and wide with Malta as their base, bringing back valuable information as to the enemy movements and intentions. Although there had been moments when the fighter defences of Malta had been overwhelmed by the superior numbers of the Italians and Germans, the arrival of the Spitfires in Malta had saved the situation, and the RAF were once again in the ascendant when he departed.

His successor was Air Vice Marshal Park, the famous officer who had commanded No. 11 Group which had taken the brunt of the German offensive in the Battle of Britain. Brigadier Sadler had worked with Air Vice Marshal Park during those days, and had often related how expertly he had handled his fighter squadrons. On the first day of the new AOC's arrival in the Island I talked with him in the fighter operations room, and I could sense at once the offensive spirit with which he was imbued. As soon as he took over command new tactics were adopted by the fighters defending Malta. In describing these tactics, and obviously making comparisons with those previously employed, it must be remembered that now, for the first time, Malta had a satisfactory number of fighters within its confines. Previously it had never possessed more than just the bare minimum necessary, so the loss of a fighter aircraft or its pilot was a serious matter for the harrassed Air Officer Commanding, and it was seldom that they could be risked very far afield from Malta's shores. Instead of waiting, as in the past, for the JU88s to cross the coast before engaging them, Air Vice Marshal Park, having organised an efficient sea rescue service, ordered his pilots to go out and meet the foe on their way in. Not only that, but he even went up himself in his own plane to see in what way these tactics could be improved. No longer were the German aeroplanes to be able to bomb the Island, and then only later worry about their safety from fighter aircraft. From now on their progress was made one of constant anxiety almost from the moment that they left the coast of Sicily. Air Vice Marshal Park publicly announced that these methods would be employed, and he also gave one or two lectures on the tactics that had been employed so successfully in the Battle of Britain. Not very long after his arrival he received the honour of a knighthood from His Majesty the King, and it is not surprising that he was immediately christened Lord Battle of Britain.

Early on in the summer Major-General Beak was posted to command a division in Egypt, and was succeeded a little time later by General Scobie, who has since become world renowned for his handling of the situation in Greece.

In June it was decided to run convoys to the relief of Malta. It was planned to sail them simultaneously from the east and from the west so that, it was hoped, the strength of the German attack would be less on each of them. However, they concentrated first of all on the convoy from Alexandria, and so prolonged were the attacks that very shortly it became clear that the ships would run out of AA ammunition long before their journey was completed. Malta had none to spare to replace what they used, and so, after suffering losses, the convoy was forced to return without reaching us. The one from the west encountered all the dangers and hazards that made the famous August Convoy so widely publicised. Out of all the ships that started only two finally struggled into the Grand Harbour. But the arrival of these two ships may possibly have saved Malta. It was learnt later from a captured officer prisoner of war that the plan to invade Malta was abandoned by the Germans after these ships had safely tied up, on the grounds that they would have brought with them sufficient quantities of armaments to replace those that they had destroyed, or imagined that they had destroyed, during their blitz in the spring.

It may well be asked whether the garrison could have resisted invasion. It was the opinion at HQ RA that the Island could have held out against the severest initial attacks. Saved specially for anti-invasion purposes were one thousand rounds per gun of all types which the CRA had carefully kept inviolate during the days of aerial attack alone. In addition to the AA armament, the Infantry Battalions were equipped with a vast preponderance of automatic weapons. Only one of the coastal defence guns had been seriously damaged, while the Field Artillery could bring down effective fire on all the beaches and inland areas. Therefore, with such fire power any combined air and sea invasion, such as was believed to be the plan of the German High Command, would have been a hazardous operation indeed. But even those reserves of ammunition would not last for ever, and if the enemy could have kept up the pressure for an indefinite period the time would have to come when the resistance of the garrison would be overwhelmed for want of shells and bullets. Whether the German staff would consider that the possession of Malta would compensate them for the enormous losses that they would sustain in such a prolonged battle was a matter that only they could decide.

During these days of June and July the aerial activity began to be stepped up once more. Massed raids were a thing of the past but high level random bombing and sharp shooting attacks by fighter bombers were frequent. Generally, also, at about 4 p.m. in the afternoon the Italians would make their token effort in the war. There is little wonder that the bombing was so inaccurate. Air Vice Marshal Park's Spitfires were harrying the Germans all the way in on their approach. As they got over the Island they were met by the full fury of the concentration of AA Artillery which helped to break up the formations that still remained, leaving stragglers and scattered units to be pounced on by our fighters once more as they returned to their bases in Sicily. The AA was now back to its normal supporting role and the kills of the RAF mounted each month. Sixty-four were brought down by the RAF alone in June and in July, they reached their zenith when, not only in defence of Malta but in victory sweeps over Sicily, they destroyed one hundred and forty-nine Axis machines. Most prominent amongst the fighter pilots at this time was Screwball Beurling. He seemed to bear a charmed existence and to be a ''dead-eyed-Dick'' with his cannon. He was a sergeant when first we knew him having just refused a commission on the grounds that if he were an officer he would have to be tidy. Later on, however, he did become an officer and we had the pleasure of his company in our Mess. Another was Wing Commander Lucas, the

Cambridge Golfing Blue who was a friend of Nick's and spent a lot of his time with us. He was greatly worried by the fact that in the Italian raids which should have been easy meat for our pilots the fighter escort was so great that they could never get in to the fat bombers. On one occasion the AA took part in this as they hit the middle 'plane, before it had dropped its bombs, which promptly blew up and destroyed the 'planes on either side of it, but this, while a reward for accurate shooting was not to be anticipated on every occasion. Laddy Lucas asked if it would be possible for the AA to continue firing instead of stopping when we saw the fighters going in as is the usual custom. We looked aghast at this but he said that he believed the chances of our hitting a fighter aircraft diving from above were very small. The Italian pilots would never take the risk whereas he was prepared to do so, and so we tried it out and most successful it proved. Larry's squadron attacked through the clouds of escorting fighters which sheared away from the AA believing that the RAF would do likewise. However, instead our 'planes held onto their course and carnage was caused amongst the Wops. To such an extent was damage done that the Italians never gave such a juicy target again to allow us to try out the tactics once more.

At night the raiding was continuous and the searchlights covered themselves with glory. An officer came out from England specially to see the work of the guns and searchlights at night. On one particular night when he was staying with us we put on the best show that could be devised as three enemy bombers were shot down by the combination of guns and searchlights. This visitor had come out also to try and help us get into the picture of the recent technical improvements in fire control that were being employed in the Air Defence of Great Britain. We had had no opportunity, through lack of the necessary instruments, of making use of these developments and we listened to him eagerly. In return he was able to profit by the experiences that we had undergone in Malta against this massed raiding by day and he was able to appreciate the makeshift arrangements that had been devised for want of more accurate instruments. But one thing did please us and that was that during the actual period of his stay with us the number of rounds that we fired for every bird "downed" happened to be less than the standard they had reached in England!

During July and the beginning of August it was obvious that a convoy would have to reach Malta soon if she was to survive. The populace were now largely feeding from communal kitchens known as Victory Kitchens. Cooks had been recruited from civil establishments and lent from military units and every assistance had been given in the way of provision of cooking utensils. All the vegetables in the Island were requisitioned by the Government to be used to provide this one meal per day at the Victory Kitchen. These meals were not very much in themselves and cost sixpence a time, but they did provide something warm and nourishing each day. Those who took advantage of these kitchens however, had to surrender a portion of their already microscopic ration. The various modes of living at this time seem very curious to look back upon. Housewives running along the street to the kitchen, queueing up to receive the little bit of vegetable soup with meat and carrying it back triumphantly to the house to consume it are sights one hopes one will never see again. But even more curious things occurred. All coinage on the Island seemed to disappear and if you bought something at a shop you received an IOU for the change unless you had taken the trouble of going to the Post Office and buying sheets of stamps for the small money. At the end of the day one would find one's pockets full with chits for change either from the Union Club or from Tony's Bar or from some Haberdashery or musical Establishment. Prices of everything had risen to undreamt of heights. There was really nothing to buy in the shops at all but if you could manage to find one needle and a reel of thread it would cost you twenty-five shillings. Eggs were two shillings and tenpence each, if you could get them. It was useless to expect to buy any kind of chicken under thirty shillings and there were not many to be had at any price. Gin was three pounds a bottle and whiskey went up to four pounds ten shillings. As always in times of crises a Black Market existed and it is said that the price of a sack of flour on this market was thirty pounds. Sugar and butter could probably be obtained at about twenty shillings a pound each. Even lime juice became so highly sought after that twenty-five shillings a bottle was an average price to pay. Money ceased to have any value.

In such conditions it was obviously necessary to try and provide some relaxation and retreat from these constant worries and so The Royal Artillery managed to obtain a part of a house belonging to the Baroness Inguanez in Mdina. This was fitted up at the direction of the CRA into an officers' club and a small allocation of spirits was obtained from the dwindling stocks of the NAAFI. Here, every Tuesday night, a dance was held for officers and their guests all of whom had to be "vetted" by an anonymous committee of ladies of the Island. But the stroke of genius in the organisation of this club was the insistence that all the ladies should wear evening dress. This was not easy for them to achieve as in many cases it meant bicycling considerable distances or returning home on foot. Many of them changed at the Club but the rule was rigorously observed and there was no doubt whatever that this return to a standard of civilisation had a most lifting effect on the morale of all who took part in it. At first there were a few protests from the inhabitants that such parties should take place. They were under the impression that rich food was being consumed within the portals of the Club, but no such thing was occurring. Parties would know that there was only a limited supply of drink at the Club and in many cases would bring their own to supplement it, and their dinners would consist of sandwiches made from the inevitable bully-beef. In fact, after a short time the population began to take heart and to reason within themselves that if such things could go on then Malta was not in so bad a way as might have been thought.

In August signs began to appear upon the roads denoting routes to numbered dumps. Preparations and rehearsals were carried out in anticipation of the arrival of a convoy. Many people knew that Malta could not hold out much longer than October, which was only six weeks away, and so the successful passage of this convoy was a matter of vital concern to every soul in the group of Islands. All the world knows the story now of the famous signal "The Convoy Must Go Through" and how the Navy and the Merchant Navy battled on with unexampled courage and determination against all the powers of the enemy. The organisation within the Island was completed down to the last detail. The ships had only to arrive when they would be instantly boarded by soldiery and Maltese stevedores. The goods would be unpacked and loaded into military trucks with special numbers for each berth, which would follow routes marked with coloured signs leading to the allotted dump. The dumps were spread out all over the Island so that the loss would not be too great if an unlucky bomb fell in the midst of a collection of stores. The Infantry, the Field and Defence Artillery supplied the military labour in connection with this unloading programme. The Coast Artillery contributed large proportions of their meagre numbers to assist also, which meant long watches for those remaining on the guns. The AA Artillery, of course, was manned to the limit as everyone anticipated a recurrence of the massed attacks but never once during the whole operation did the enemy approach the Island. Fighter aircraft took the air in the very early hours of each day as the convoy approached, Beau-fighters to give them protection far afield from Malta and Spit-fires when they came within the operational range of these tiny planes. Eventually as all the world knows out of seventeen ships three only at first dropped anchor under the barraccas of Valetta and Senglea. It looked as though Malta was lost. But battling on with her bows almost awash, her back broken, and subjected to constant attacks, was the tanker "Ohio". The morning after the arrival of the three ships we all rubbed our eyes with amazement for there, steaming round the south-west corner of the Island was a large Merchant Ship apparently unscathed. She had been involved in an E boat attack, had had to go out of her course to avoid it and had lost the convoy. So the captain decided to take her over and shelter under the Tunisian coast. This he did during the hours of daylight and as dark fell he set course again for Malta to bring his ship in as a heaven-sent and welcome addition to the trio that had arrived. Meanwhile with our hearts in our mouths we followed the progress of the "Ohio" for two days as she slowly approached the Island. It did not seem possible that she would ever be able to make port but the determination of her captain, Captain Mason, and of the destroyer commanders who lashed their ships to either side of the stricken tanker won through in the end. The day after the arrival of the lone ship, the "Ohio" to the accompaniment of frantic applause and the heightened emotions of all, wallowed, no other word can express it, past Elmo Lighthouse into the placid waters of the Grand Harbour. Her cargo of vital oil and petrol was almost the most precious of all. With her arrival the operation could be said to have been a success. Now there was sufficient fuel to work the pumps that supplied the water to the Island. Air Vice Marshal Park's fighters had more petrol now with which to operate and the Island became less dependent on those gallant exploits of HM Submarines whereby they crept under the surface, with petrol tanks strapped to their sides and with their torpedo tubes crammed full of supplies, to bring relief to the beleaguered garrison. It is nice to record that Captain Mason's modesty was as great as his courage. When he came to lunch in our Mess and we took him for a tour of the Island to whose safety he had contributed so greatly, we asked him what his reactions were. His reply was immediate "I want to come on the next trip and get my tanker in whole this time".

CHAPTER XII

Reprise

But the arrival of the convoy was, alas, no panacea for all the ills of Malta. Many people thought now that the days of plenty had come again, and that the need for scrupulous care in the handling of rations was a thing of the past. Lord Gort, with infinite wisdom and judgment, immediately disillusioned all such wishful thinkers. He broadcast to the populace over the redif-fusion system very shortly after the 'ships had arrived, saying we must look on these supplies purely as a means whereby the target date could be put further forward into the limbo of the future. There was no denying that this caused grave distress to the popu-lation, who had anticipated better things, but the wisdom of his ' judgment was amply borne out by the slender margin which existed in Malta when relief finally came. And so throughout the month of September the civilians and soldiers alike struggled on without gas, without electricity, with little fuel, and with very little food and with none of the ordinary relaxations, such as the cinema or the theatre, with which they could take their minds away from the grim spectres that assailed them. Even beer, that staple requirement of all soldiers, was impossible to obtain. There was no power to work the brewery, even had there been the hops with which to make the beer. When later on at last it proved possible to start brewing beer once more only one of the firms able to do so in Malta could be allowed to operate. Unfor-tunately, on the opening day one of the Maltese workmen fell into the vat and was drowned, and the rival firm was libellously alleged to have put the story about that this was the first time there had been any malt in the other firm's beer.

There was really nothing for anyone to do apart from work-ing, bathing and taking as little out of one's self as possible in order to have some reserve left for any future days of strain. Even cleanliness was a problem owing to the non-existence of any hot water. Many ways of producing heat were tried, of which flash cookers, a combination of water and old engine oil as an inflammable mixture, proved the most efficacious. The least successful was an attempt to burn seaweed, which only resulted in a particularly nasty smell of iodine. Luckily it was summer, and summers in Malta are hot, so cold showers were no hardship. At least we did not suffer from that acute water shortage that soldiers in the desert endured. There was plenty of water in those underground wells if the fuel for the pumping machinery was always available.

It is in times like these that the Maltese nation turns to its faith for support and courage. The regiments of the Royal Malta Artillery were no exception to this rule. Perhaps it was to gain strength for the ordeal that they were facing, or perhaps it was to give their soldiers something definite to think about, or even perhaps it was a gesture of Christian defiance against the heathen precepts of Nazism—maybe it was a combination of them all that led to a series of the most inspiring and beautiful religious ceremonies in each regiment. Each unit in turn held a service of dedication to its patron saint. These services varied from the panoply and colour of the dedication of the Coast Regiment by the Archbishop-Bishop in the historic chapel of Fort St. Elmo to homely services in a tiny chapel in Zeitun. They would be followed by a ceremonial parade and by the lavish hospitality that is an integral part of any Maltese occasion. It was a fine method of renewing the soldier's faith in his God and in his unit, and none who were fortunate enough to attend could fail to be impressed by the sincerity of the ceremony. They were truly a source of strength for the trials to come.

But if the sands of time were running low for Malta, they were now beginning to run out for the enemy in Africa. Generals Alexander and Montgomery were now installed in the Middle East theatre, and had already beaten off Rommel's attempt to break through to the Suez Canal. Now they were building up those vast reserves of stores and ammunition preparatory to the great offensive that was so urgently needed to prise the enemy from Egyptian soil. The two rival armies faced each other across the sand dunes of El Alamein in the lull that always precedes the breaking of the storm. All through the summer Malta had aided by proving a troublesome neighbour to the Axis. Almost as soon as the weight of attack lifted she began once again to assert her offensive powers, and many were the ships that were sunk en route to the North African ports from their bases in Sicily and Italy.

It has been said that Rommel and Kesselring held divergent views on the advisability of invading Malta or not. Kesselring is alleged to have advised Rommel to stop on the Egyptian frontier during his pursuit of the Eighth Army and to take Malta, thus securing his lines of communication. Rommel clung to the military principle of maintenance of the objective. His objective was Cairo and Alexandria, and to take Malta would mean a diversion and a loss in time which would give the British an opportunity to recover. If he pressed on he might get right through to the precious Suez Canal and become master of the Near East. How nearly he succeeded is support for the correctness of his view. But over eighty thousand tons of shipping were sunk by offensive sorties from Malta, which may well prove how right Kesselring was in his appreciation of the situation. Whoever was correct, the Germans now realised that they could not afford to have their lines of communication harried and menaced by aeroplanes and submarines from Malta while they were resisting the inevitable offensive of General Montgomery, and so Malta once more resounded to its theme song of bombs and barrage.

In the middle of October Kesselring flung in his last desperate attempt to annihilate that Mediterranean Island. It began by an attack at dusk. General Beckett, whose promotion to Major-General had been announced during the summer to the delight of all, was about to leave Luqa aerodrome for a visit to the AA defences of the Middle East. Brigadier Clark (who succeeded Brigadier Hire in command of the Heavy AA Brigade when the latter was appointed Brigadier AA of the 9th Army) with Brigadiers White and Woolley and myself had all gone up to the aerodrome to see him off. The air alarm was sounded, but this was nothing unusual, and no bombing raid had materialised by day for some weeks. However, this was a raid in earnest, and almost before we had time to think all three Brigadiers and myself were lying flat on the tarmac under the wing of the Liberator plane which was the only four-engined aircraft on the aerodrome, and therefore became the centre of the attack. General Beckett himself was inside the aeroplane with the rest of the crew, and there they remained throughout the raid. Bombs seemed to fall everywhere except actually on us, and it was a very frightening experience. But perhaps the most alarming moments were when a small arms dump began to explode about one hundred yards away to our left. Bullets whistled in every direction, and there was no telling where was the safest place to avoid them. Almost by a miracle none of us was hurt, nor was the raid very effective.

This was the beginning of one of the most exciting weeks in Malta's history. The Germans flung in every ounce of strength that they could, but they were out-fought and out-matched by the tactics of Air Vice Marshal Park's fighters and the co-operation of the AA Artillery. Right out almost to Sicily did the Air Vice Marshal send his Spitfires, and he had built them up to such numbers that they presented a formidable attacking force even when splitting into three as was done this time. The first group of fighters, as already stated, met the bombers coming in. Then the AA opened up on them as they approached the coast and crossed it, and broke up their formations. Over the island itself a second force of fighters was ready to dash into the fray, and finally, as the stricken enemy began to flee for home, the third group of fighters, which had been waiting for this moment, tore in to destroy them. In one week one hundred and eighteen enemy planes were destroyed by these tactics. It was the RAF's field day and to them goes the glory of the victory. As we said in a message to them, we had Jerries first eleven against us and it was their turn to bat. They certainly hit the enemy bowling all over the field, and the spirit in which our message was sent was reciprocated by the graceful acknowledgement of the co-operation of the AA Artillery with which Air Vice Marshal Park replied. During that month of October, one hundred and forty-one 'planes were destroyed, of which the RAF claimed one hundred and thirty-two and the AA nine. But the score in "kills" is no criterion of the respective efforts. All that mattered was that the combined defences of Malta had routed the enemy.

This was the end of the Luftwaffe over Malta. Apart from one more evening raid in late December, which, by a lucky chance, hit a Wellington loaded up with bombs causing damage to others, this was the last appearance of the German airforce over Malta in strength. The battle had been long and hard and as is the way of most dangerous and treacherous reptiles, the last thrust was almost the most dangerous. But they had been forced to cry quits and admit defeat, and from that moment on Malta was left severely alone. In all, during the months to which she had been subjected to attack, eleven thousand one hundred and thirty-four bombers had crossed the Island's coast and unloaded a total of sixteen thousand five hundred and fifty tons of bombs. Of this number of 'planes, one thousand two hundred had been destroyed by the end of 1942, which shows what a high total was exacted by the defences as a whole.

In many ways this last onslaught must have been the severest trial of all to the Maltese. It came after a long period of comparative inactivity by day when, perhaps, they might have been forgiven for thinking that the days of sudden and violent death had departed and gone. As it was, the full force of this attack struck them when they were almost at the lowest level of their powers of physical resistance. The prolonged starvation had begun to leave its mark and it is so much easier to be brave if one has a full stomach. Similarly, if one is hungry how easy it is to let depression and despair get the better of one's reserves of physical courage. And so I would like to quote just two incidents, both of which took place just at this time, which illustrate the spirit of the people. I was standing in that little Antique Shop in Kingsway kept by that well-known character Carmela, whom some will remember as the old lady who led the crowd out of the shelter, crossing herself as she stepped into the sunlight, in the film called "George Cross Malta." I was buying a length of lovely material to send home as a Christmas present and the wireless was playing in the back. Just as we were discussing it Carmela ceased to take part in the transaction and stood rigidly to attention. At first I did not appreciate what had happened and then suddenly I realised that from the wireless in the back room came the strains of the National Anthem at the end of one of the programmes. As soon as the last notes died away Carmela relaxed and returned to business.

Up in Rabat there is a famous shop which sells Malta lace and Malta cloth. It had been bombed during the summer and one of the children of the helpers in the shop had been killed. I was trying to buy some small Christmas presents for Wendy. When I had completed my purchases I happened to mention that she was six. The lady turned to me and said, "I would so like you to have this little pinafore. It was to be for the child that we lost, but I'm sure your baby would like to have it."

If, in the midst of all the adversity, hardship and danger that had afflicted these people, one could meet with a spontaneous spirit like that, one need have no doubt of the greatness that lies within.

CHAPTER XIII

Finale

Some dramas build up to a magnificent climax in which everything happens in the last two minutes of the play. The loose ends are tidied up and a spectacular curtain puts paid to the scene. Others end on a quieter note. Playgoers and readers of this book may remember that enchanting production in London of Jerome Kern's "The Cat and the Fiddle". In the last scene the story was ended, the lovers reunited and the play and the music slipped quietly and gently to their close. It was over. And yet so unconventional was this ending that few were prepared for it. So it was with Malta. The relief of Malta did not depend entirely on the thunderous barrage or the dashing tactics of the fighters. It depended much more on the long looked for triumph of Alamein and the safe arrival of a convoy in the Grand Harbour. It was food and supplies that were badly needed and they could not be got to the Island until bases for air protection had been established along the northern shores of Africa. And so the defeat of the Luftwaffe in that ·October battle, although it brought great relief to all when it was finally realised that they had retired from the fray, was not the moment on which the curtain could be rung down on the drama in triumph. There were still weeks of starvation and fatigue to be faced. Preparations had to be made for the reception of ships that, if El Alamein was not successful, would never sail to Malta. It was fully realised that it would be asking too much to expect another operation from the West, such as the August convoy, with its enormous losses to both the Merchant Navy and the fighting units of the Royal Navy.

And so everyone cast about for ways in which relief could be found from the anxieties of these days. For a long time now each Artillery Brigade had had a concert party composed of its members which had toured all the gun positions and even given performances in the big halls in Valetta and elsewhere. The standard reached by each of these parties was something to be marvelled at. The Heavy AA Brigade Concert Party was fortunate in having two well-known professional pianists and a magnificent operatic tenor in its cast, while the high-light of the Light AA Brigade Party was its choir of Welsh singers from the Welsh Searchlight Battery that we had in Malta. These parties had been constantly rehearsing and performing for months but now, in response to the call for entertainment and relaxation they redoubled their efforts, sometimes giving two or three performances each day. In addition to this light entertainment courses of instruction in all sorts of hobbies, handicrafts and studies, were organised for the troops and everything possible with the limited resources available was devised to keep them occupied and amused.

Colonel Ellis who, since being wounded by a bomb, had had to be invalided out of the Army had again taken up his original employment of Manager of the Rediffusion Company. He came to me and asked me if I could devise any series of theatrical entertainment or broadcasts that could be of use for the troops. We tried hard, and under K Warren's direction we got "Springtime For Henry" into rehearsal with Nick and I playing the roles in which Nigel Bruce and Ronald Squire respectively had scored such successes. Messrs. Samuel French, in response to an appeal from me saying that the play was to be produced at our own expense and free to soldier audiences only, very graciously waived any question of royalties, for which we were more than grateful. But fate willed against it as, just as it was taking shape, General Beckett was appointed to a command at home and so Nick and I had to give up our roles so as to be available to help the new CRA get into the picture. With its tiny cast, one set and rather robust humour it would have been a good production with which to tour the gun positions and Infantry localities.

Meanwhile I was also trying to see what could be done in the way of broadcasts. In this I was more than fortunate in that firstly, our Intelligence Officer was now Kenneth Darke (a nephew of the famous organist) who was a concert pianist of brilliant ability and secondly, living only a few hundred yards away in Mdina was Ada Bonello. I met her one day walking along the street and almost before I had time to think I found myself asking her if she would come and sing and do a series of broadcasts. I was rather afraid that she would find it difficult to get away from her duties as wife and mother but she made light of these and said that there would be nothing that she would not do to try and help.

And so a series of broadcasts was devised based on the evidence contained in my "Parker's Theatrical Who's Who."

In each broadcast, which lasted about thirty-five to forty minutes, we took a famous star of the light musical stage, tracing her career from the moment that she began right up till the latest news that we had of her and illustrating it with songs that she had sung from each of the shows. This may sound easy, but it certainly was not. It meant going round to one's friends and asking permission to burrow through their music to discover if they had a particular piece of music from a certain show. Very often if they had the music they had not got the words, and so it meant pestering other friends to remember the words of the songs and sometimes, I regret to state, we made up new lyrics which were broadcast without any kind permission of any author except myself. Ada would come down for first rehearsal each Tuesday probably never having heard of the songs she had got to sing on the following Monday. We would peg away at these until at last we had a rough idea of each of the songs. Then I would write the script and Ken would work on the musical arrangements of the accompaniments. In addition I persuaded him to play many solo pieces, some of them I fancy rather to his sorrow after his previous standard of Bach and Beethoven. Two more rehearsals and a final run through brought us to the day of the broadcast. It was close timing. Amongst the stars whose lives were thus portrayed were Peggy Wood, Evelyn Laye, Dorothy Dickson, Lea Seidl, Edith Day and Mary Ellis, but there were others too, and the series continued for some months. Should any of them read these pages they need have no fear about what was said. Everything was painted in the most glowing colours and whenever possible we used the original records that they had made themselves. But how few of these there were after the blitz was soon discovered and eventually the burden of almost all the songs fell on Ada.

Just as the series was due to commence with herself as the first "victim" I received a copy from America of Peggy Wood's autobiography "How Young You Look." We had been friends for years, Peggy and I, and I had also had the privilege of accompanying her on the piano while she sang some of the songs from that exquisite operetta "Bitter Sweet" of which she had been the unforgettably lovely heroine. She had been a most faithful correspondent and it was with intense pleasure that I found she had included extracts from letters of mine telling of our efforts to keep drama alive in Malta. What with BBC broadcasts and writes-up in Peggy's book the MADC was getting famous.

This seemed a good omen but even so we approached the first broadcast with considerable trepidation. This was a new

line of country that had not yet been attempted by the
Rediffusion Company or by ourselves, and it was not made
easier by the sounding of the air alarm as we went up to the
microphone in the improvised studio we were using near Manoel
Island. Ada, who truth to tell was terrified of air-raids, just
looked at me, I made a re-assuring face at her and, reacting like
the great "trouper" she is, she proceeded to sing like an angel.
But perhaps my greatest memory of her was during the singing
of that pathetic song from Frederica "Why Did You Kiss My
Heart Awake." Ada was a person who was terribly nervous of any
kind of an audience and she was particularly frightened of this
song, which I thought she sang to perfection. Owing to a technical
hitch we were a little short of time on this broadcast and it was
the last number in the programme. We were to be followed by a
comedy team from the RAF Concert Party and we were broadcasting from makeshift premises owing to the others having
been destroyed. Just as she got well into the song this team of
comedians with their props came into the room and began to
assemble very quietly right opposite where she was singing. I
felt certain that Ada's nerves would get the better of her and that
the climax of the broadcast would be spoilt. Instead of that, she
threw her whole soul into the pathos of the song and that
particular broadcast was the most widely acclaimed of all the
series that we did. In the very last series I managed to persuade
her, very much against her will, to do a broadcast of Malta
memories, listing all the best songs from plays that she had
played lead in in Malta, and in addition she was good enough to
include in it a song that I had specially written for her to sing
at some concerts that she gave for the troops in addition to the
programme of broadcasts. At the end Colonel Ellis came to the
microphone unexpectedly and expressed his appreciation of the
series that we had performed. It was a gesture for which we
were all very grateful and certainly Ada and Ken deserved all
the eulogies that he lavished upon them. But we were sad
because our final project had to be abandoned. We had devised
an adaptation for broadcasting of "Bitter Sweet" and we had
been greatly strengthened in our resolve by the fact that when
the project was referred to Noel Coward, he had generously
replied that although he had never previously allowed any
shortened version of "Bitter Sweet" to be performed, he would
gladly give permission for this adaptation to be broadcast. In
addition, as a gesture of admiration to the Island, he would
waive all his author's royalties for the performances. Alas, time
was too short for all the intensive rehearsing that would have
been involved and we had to abandon the idea as I was leaving
Malta soon.

But long before the last of these broadcasts had been given, El Alamein had been fought and won and Rommel and his forces were being hurled pell mell out of Egypt and Libya. Air bases were established in record time along the coast of Africa and in the middle of November, early one morning, four ships arrived from the Middle East, having met no opposition of any kind on their way. It seemed incredible to think that four fat merchant ships had really arrived. No news of sorties by the Italian battle-fleet or attacks by submarines or aircraft had heralded their arrival. No thunderous barrage roared out in protection and welcome as they negotiated that last turn past Elmo light-house. In fact, so well was the secret of their arrival kept, that very few of the civilians had an inkling of their approach. The inhabitants of Valetta, Senglea and Floriana woke up one morning and rubbed their eyes with amazement. Four ships were in harbour where none had been the night before. Already they were being unloaded. In the nick of time as only a few days more rations were available in the depots. Malta had been relieved.

From now on the passage from Alexandria was to become almost a matter of a fortnightly routine run. Ships came in, were unloaded, stayed waiting a day or so and then left under the protection of the escort that had just brought in their successors. But again His Excellency the Governor was careful to make sure there was no prodigal expenditure of the precious stores that had arrived. Even for Christmas there was very little extra allocation in actual food. The extra "dollop" consisted of a quarter of a pound of beans and two candles per person. The Maltese never lost their sense of humour and immediately the joke went round, "How are you feeling after Christmas?" "Grand thanks. I'm full of beans."

But Christmas was to bring with it a loss to the Island. General Beckett who had led the Royal Artillery and the Royal Malta Artillery throughout the worst months of the battle of Malta was given a new command at home and was to be succeeded by General Christie. To those of us on his staff, his loss was a sad one indeed. Working for him had meant working at full pressure at all times, but he never hesitated to give praise where praise was due, or to listen attentively to the ideas of any of his subordinates. It was his strength of personality that had welded the gunners into one cohesive force that had united to its highest efficiency in the moments of crisis for the defence of the fortress. One of the occasions which I know he looked back on with most pride was the parade he organised on St. Barbara's day, the patron saint of gunners. It was then that could be seen by all the intense pride that each gunner in that Island took in belonging to the brotherhood of the Royal Artillery. And I know that he appreciated the fact that all ranks considered that he was largely the author of that pride.

General Christie asked George Wishart and me to remain with him on his staff until he could be firmly in the saddle and thus it was that we were enabled to be present three months later at a march past of the Royal Malta Artillery through the streets of Valetta at which His Excellency the Governor took the salute. Every Unit had representative detachments on parade and the magnificent bearing of the men was eloquent testimony to the high standard of morale and discipline that had been maintained in the most adverse circumstances. The civil populace turned out en masse to greet each contingent with waving flags, cheering and clapping. But the biggest reception of all was reserved for H. E. himself when he stepped down from the saluting base in front of the ruined palace of Valetta, and we who remained saw him nearly mobbed as he made his triumphant progress to his waiting car. It was most inspiring to see the enthusiasm and the loyalty with which he was greeted, for although Malta had been snatched from the jaws of disaster the measures that he had been forced to employ had been drastic in the extreme on the civilian population. This spectacular march through the ruined streets of Valetta was a stirring finale for George and me, as it came right at the end of our sojourn in Malta as we were preparing to hand over to our successors.

Saying good-bye is always a sad affair and these good-byes were even harder to say than usual. After four years Malta had become a home and it was a wrench to leave all the familiar surroundings. Farewell parties there were in profusion, both private and official. The pleasant words that were spoken at the latter and the feelings of friendship expressed at both will always be for me a grateful memory. If I single out any one function it is not because it was better than any of the others but because it was given by the original unit of the Royal Malta Artillery, the first Coast Regiment, at their magnificent Mess at Fort St. Elmo. Here the first bomb had fallen and the first military casualties had occurred. From that regiment had sprung two Heavy AA Regiments, one Light AA Regiment, a second Coast Artillery Regiment, a Searchlight Battery, and a Defence Artillery Battery. Officers had been drawn in great numbers from that parent unit in the early days of the war. After only a month or six weeks of training in AA Artillery, they had been sent out to isolated gun positions and told to carry on. They and the men under them had done a grand job. They

Field Marshal Lord Gort, Governor and Commander-in-Chief, followed by Maj-Gen Oxley, GOC Troops Malta; Maj-Gen Christie, CRA Malta and their respective Staff Officers proceed to inspect the Royal Malta Artillery parade in March 1943.

fought back with all they had got and now, even more than before, will the Royal Malta Artillery be the pride of its homeland.

In the second week of April, after a farewell cocktail party in my flat (on the proceeds of a carefully guarded collection that had been specially reserved for just this purpose) followed by a terrific dining-out in our Mess, I was driven in the early hours of the morning to the aerodrome at Luqa in company with Nick and George, who was to leave himself a day or so later. A few farewells were said and I told them to go back quickly. There are moments when one would rather be alone. It had been four years almost to the day that I had landed in Malta, together with the first reinforcements ever sent to its defence. I was leaving one week after the first reduction in the garrison in all those years. The Malta Infantry Brigade, which was soon to earn new laurels in Sicily and Italy had left to prepare and train for the arduous tasks ahead of them. The Island, whose reserves had once been so low, was now fully provisioned again. There had been many occasions on which life had been difficult, desperate and almost overwhelmingly complicated, but in sum it was good to look back upon and to feel that one had contributed a small quota to history by having participated in those years of siege and bombardment.

After their car had disappeared in the cloud of dust and I had recovered from my bout of nostalgia I realised that there might be a lengthy wait and so when Brigadier Clark of the Heavy AA Brigade drove up to say goodbye I was as pleased as I was flattered. Even better, I went back with him to a second breakfast as the 'plane was not likely to take off for another hour. With this last kind gesture of hospitality from that always hospitable HQ I bade goodbye to him and his staff and returned to the aerodrome.

The sun was shining and the air was still crisp and cool as the Liberator taxied slowly along to the head of the runway. Malta was at its most beautiful. Under a canopy of blue sky the russet church towers and domes were just beginning to shed themselves of the purple early morning haze, revealing the yellow ochre colouring of the massive structures they surmounted. Nestling beneath them were the colourful little villages, like collections of so many toy bricks, so familiar and yet, in these last moments, so strangely distant. Civita Vecchia reared its lofty magnificence to the heavens—a symbol of strength and solidarity—its beauty in the early morning sun only challenged by the memories of its pale loveliness by moonlight.

The engines increased their roar, the ground slipped by, and imperceptibly we took the air. Looking down I saw below us Hal Far with its memories of Faith, Hope and Charity; Luqa, the home of bombers and fighters; Safi, where so many gunners had fought back so desperately against raids on aerodromes on either side of them and in front of them; Ta Kali, the home of the fighters that finally put paid to the Luftwaffe; Krendi, that brand new aerodrome constructed in the teeth of enemy attacks; and lastly, as we banked again the outline of the Grand Harbour and Manoel Island came into view. What memories there were in that small space. "Illustrious" battling for her life, convoys unloading their precious cargo, barrages rending the air, the empty shells of houses in Valetta, the Submarine Base from where those long lean craft had never ceased to harry the enemy; Manoel Island itself with its ruined gun pits testifying to the gallantry of the men who had served there even unto death; and lastly the ruins of Tigne Barracks, for so long packed with guns which had hurled defiance against the foe attacking both by air and by sea.

We climbed again and circled round for the last time. There below in a sea of sapphire blue lay a little island of emerald green, proud, defiant and triumphant.

CHAPTER XIV

Epilogue

Malta had certainly passed through the valley of the shadow of death, and was already glimpsing the bright horizon beyond, but none could have foreseen in that month of April how soon the wheel of fate would turn full circle. The visit of His Majesty the King to the Island on which he had conferred his own award was yet to come. Generals Eisenhower, Alexander and Montgomery had not yet established their headquarters on that bomb-scarred soil. The Prime Minister of Great Britain had yet to see its battered battlements, and nor would anyone then have dreamt that the Great President of the United States of America was to fly there specially to pay a gracious and generous tribute. Instead of being invaded Malta was to launch the invasion against the home shores of the Axis. With what a sense of drama was Fate to select the anniversary of the relief of the first siege of Malta for the passage of the surrendered Italian Fleet past the historic bastions of Fort St. Elmo into the waters of the very harbour they had tried so desperately to acquire.

If any glory can recompense a nation for the scars of war Malta has truly earned and been granted her reward.

3766. 7-46. 500